'An enjoyable and refreshing take on major trends and changes that leaders must successfully embrace if they are to ensure that they succeed in their career. This book provides thought-provoking insights, research and advice that all leaders should actively consider.'

Helen Gordon, Chief Executive, Science Council

'This book blends scholarly research and practice-based insights to force a rethink of what ongoing social shifts, enterprise innovations and altering societal values imply for future careers.'

Alnoor Bhimani, Professor of Management Accounting & Director of South Asia Centre, London School of Economics

'As this book sets out, leading is an activity not a label. The authors set out a compelling vision for a more people-centred, impact-led approach to navigate the "next normal".'

Gwen Hines, CEO, Save the Children UK

'An inspiring and highly energizing read which enables us to take stock of where we are, and where we want to go in our careers. This book decodes complex and accelerating changes in the world around us and brings a refreshing way to think about how we develop ourselves, our teams and our workplaces.'

Erem Kassim-Lakha, Partner, McKinsey & Company

FUTUREPROOF YOUR CAREER

How to Lead and Succeed in
A CHANGING WORLD

Shaheena Janjuha-Jivraj & Naeema Pasha

BLOOMSBURY BUSINESS
LONDON · OXFORD · NEW YORK · NEW DELHI · SYDNEY

BLOOMSBURY BUSINESS
Bloomsbury Publishing Plc
50 Bedford Square, London, WC1B 3DP, UK
29 Earlsfort Terrace, Dublin 2, Ireland

BLOOMSBURY, BLOOMSBURY BUSINESS and the Diana logo are trademarks
of Bloomsbury Publishing Plc

First published in Great Britain 2021

A catalogue record for this book is available from the British Library

Library of Congress Cataloguing-in-Publication data has been applied for

ISBN: 978-1-4729-8844-7; eBook: 978-1-4729-8838-6

2 4 6 8 10 9 7 5 3 1

Typeset by Deanta Global Publishing Services, Chennai, India
Printed and bound in Great Britain by CPI Group (UK) Ltd, Croydon CR0 4YY

To find out more about our authors and books visit www.bloomsbury.com
and sign up for our newsletters

We dedicate this book to our students, colleagues and friends who have inspired us, and to our families who have supported us throughout the writing process.

For Surinder and Amina, Iliyan, Kais and Zayn, from deep roots grow strong branches. SJJ

To my wonderful family and friends who remind me that the little things in life are actually the big things. NP

Contents

Introduction

The world of work is a place filled with so many opportunities for you to immerse yourself in – to jump in, contribute, shape and lead. There's no doubt this decade gives us an exciting time to think about work and changes that are happening. When we consider the specific impact of new technology on work, the shifts we are already experiencing and are likely to experience over the next five to 10 years, so much of what we are used to will be transformed. A fair amount will seemingly be at a visible level – how we consume technology, hybrid working (hybrid working is when work is carried out as a blend of home working and workplace working), adapting into distributed organizations and leadership styles. Other elements of change are more deep-rooted and far less visible but equally, if not more, impactful on how we will work and what we will focus on. In this book we dig deep in these areas to help you make sense of the changes that are happening at such a fast speed and equip you with the thinking and knowledge to prepare the next steps in your career. Our position is that each of you is vested, not only in your career but in developing your leadership capabilities to bring about change and become an agent in this workplace transformation. This new era of work, the next normal, demanded very different leadership skills and we introduce entrepreneurial leadership as a way of creating talented pluralistic teams together to anticipate change and innovate and transform.

Before we jump into the contents of this book further, we want to share why we, Shaheena and Naeema, wrote this book together. This book is the result of a four-year journey. As colleagues, we were both delivering on a week-long programme for 'Women in Leadership in Emerging Tech'. After we delivered our sessions on the future of work and leadership capabilities, we reflected on the sessions and the conversations emerging from this group of highly talented individuals sharing their views on workplace changes as a result of tech integration. The points ranged from the impact of implementing deep learning (IBM Watson) to governance around data handling and decision making, and ethical issues on how data was accumulated and deployed. As we continued to work together on teaching programmes, conversations kept coming back to how individuals understand the impact of change that is upon us and more importantly, their reactions. We were seeing so many dynamic individuals who are clearly an asset to their organization but who hadn't had the opportunity to step back and comprehend the ramifications of change in their roles and organizations, and more importantly, for their careers. Despite writing numerous articles for *Forbes* and other publications, including *Management Today* and *HR Magazine*, and delivering keynote speeches, webinars and podcasts across this area, we wanted the opportunity to dive deep into this area to give our readers the chance to break down these big, complex issues and really consider what these mean on an individual level. As we discuss the impact of new technology, artificial intelligence (AI) and the fourth industrial revolution, the future of work, reskilling as our currency for renewal and relevancy, the need to rethink leadership with a more entrepreneurial approach, there is a thread that runs across all of these areas for every individual: your relationship with work, your responsibility to invest in your career and your opportunity to develop the necessary skills and step into leadership.

What happens when two leaders who are problem solvers and innovators identify a challenge? We grasped the opportunity to start mapping out a solution. This book was written during the height of the coronavirus pandemic in 2020, which provided an opportunity to step back and speak to a fantastic array of business leaders to understand the ramifications of this turbulence to the workplace. One unexpected but powerful outcome from this process was diversity of thinking between us as authors; on the surface we're pretty similar – female (tick), Asian (tick), work in academia (tick), but our educational disciplines and career experiences brought so much difference to how we addressed topics – and this was a powerful reminder of the importance and benefits when you let cognitive diversity thrive in generating new ideas.

What is it about the two of us that makes this a compelling read?

Shaheena is Associate Professor in Entrepreneurial Leadership and Gender Diversity at HEC Paris in Qatar. She combines her areas of expertise – innovation, diversity and leadership – to help students and organizations rethink how they can encourage different approaches in building cultures and teams. Having taught entrepreneurship for a number of years and set up two entrepreneurship centres at business schools in the UK, she recognized the gap in understanding the need to improve cognitive diversity and nurturing cultures to create optimal conditions for innovation. She has delivered leadership training programmes to thousands of individuals and has worked with global companies across a range of sectors, including engineering, transport, banking and finance, manufacturing, retailing, non-governmental organizations (NGOs) and charities. Shaheena encourages individuals to recognize that leadership behaviours occur at any point in the organization and can create powerful new services and products. The impact of her work has reached more than 53 countries at policy level, working with the UK Cabinet office, the Commonwealth Secretariat and the EU. Shaheena is a *Forbes* contributor and this is her third book.

Naeema is Director of Careers and Founder of World of Work (WOW) at Henley Business School and with her team, the recipient of multiple awards for careers services. A big part of this success is down to Naeema's vision in transforming careers support for students across the business school beyond simply matching students to roles, instead creating agency for their careers, using creative approaches to encourage them to get out of their comfort zone and realize their capability to stretch and build resilience. A few examples include training students to deliver comedy (if you've ever done this for colleagues, you will know how nerve-wracking it can be). Her doctoral research on the future of work, completed in 2019 (which went under the title of 'A Study of Career Resilience, Personality and Competencies in the Context of Career Uncertainty and Future of Work'), has propelled her expertise and thinking into this area to be acknowledged by senior leaders, considered leaders in the space of new tech and work, leading to Naeema being named as one of the IFPC-online Top 50 Worldwide Influencers on AI Ethics in 2020. Naeema founded the World of Work (WOW) forum in 2017, creating a platform that sees thousands of participants engaging hundreds of companies with educators and students to use data and evidence to consider how social and technological change impacts how we work. She has also been appointed as Leadership Fellow at the Society of Leadership Fellow, St George's House, Windsor Castle, a society set up by HRH Duke of Edinburgh in 1966 for leaders to come together to consider the bigger questions in society. Her views are regularly included in industry reports, most recently the Microsoft future trends reports of 2020.

Enough about us, let's turn to you. What are you hoping to get from this book? Well, as a starting point, we hope you will feel even more excited and optimistic about how your career and leadership aspirations will unfold. In understanding the opportunities and challenges emerging from new tech, you can break down the ambiguity into digestible pieces. There are three things we aim for you to take away from this book:

1) As you learn more about specific areas of emerging and frontier technology, you develop a deeper understanding of how it will shape you, your work and your leadership. You will find ways to understand how to be more motivated

and inspired to find out more and bring this knowledge into your work – whether this is getting involved in creative thinking, data-driven initiatives, or both.

2) You know that you are the driver for your career, and OK, you'll know serendipity plays a role in all of our lives, but you will also see that the more you define your path, the greater the chances of success. This isn't about goal setting in the traditional sense, more about you being clear on your drivers and motivations and recognizing the choice of paths you can take to achieve your plans and create your legacy. And ultimately, knowing you can create the future you want.

3) Getting comfortable with leadership and recognizing your entrepreneurial leadership capabilities will enable you to achieve the changes you want, wherever you are in the organization, rather than waiting five or 10 years until you reach the upper echelons of the organization. Of course, with this leadership opportunity, there is great responsibility but this reinforces why strong drivers and commitment are so important and why you are the person leading on this particular initiative.

As you contemplate these three areas there is a common thread and it comes down to getting out of your comfort zone, welcoming the opportunity to learn new skills and different ways of thinking. The more you challenge yourself to stretch, the greater the benefits that emerge through resilience and taking on new opportunities.

This book is split into two sections: the first two chapters provide the big, overarching areas – macro trends in work, the impact of the global pandemic coupled with technology transformation. In Chapter 3, we provide a deeper dive into new technologies; this is really useful for the non-techie among you and we've pulled out the main trends that we know are impacting work in the immediate future. Even if you are familiar with all of these areas, you will find it useful to consider how you can bring in colleagues by using some of the thinking and examples in this chapter. In Chapter 4, we open the conversation to discuss how entrepreneurial leadership is the leadership approach for moving through turbulence, uncertainty and change in organizations.

The second part of the book is more specific to you and your career development; in Chapter 5, we emphasize the importance of resilience specifically for your career. Then in Chapter 6, we discuss key elements of diversity that need to be addressed to unlock innovation and handle the implications of technology in teams. We focus on the imperative to create pluralistic cultures in teams by removing groupthink and biases and discuss some of the key challenges around ethics and new technology. Chapter 7 focuses on data and its growing importance as a tool for leaders to understand how to handle data as an invaluable means to identify trends and make decisions with more certainty. Chapter 8 explains how career dynamism provides the springboard for your career in fast-moving organizations. As reskilling and ongoing knowledge acquisition become our essential resources, in Chapter 9 we provide insights into learning and how traditional, formal education can create mindset barriers and what you can do to remove those blockers. In Chapter 10, we provide insights into proven ways to propel your career forwards. Some of these ideas emerge from work in the diversity space and are useful for more senior leaders to identify ways to increase the pipeline of diverse talent. Finally, Chapter 11 is a round-up to help you pull the pieces together again.

You don't need to follow the order we have suggested – we do cross-reference chapters so if you dive straight into the middle then you have indications of what's going on in other chapters.

We've written this book to trigger thinking and throughout, we ask you questions and encourage you to consider your reactions, your plans. Whether you are reading or listening to this book, imagine that we are having a conversation and asking you these questions, so we really encourage you to take the time and answer them, grab your phone, laptop, tablet or quill to make notes and diary reminders to review your answers where we suggest time periods.

Enjoy – and get comfortable with becoming uncomfortable!

Shaheena & Naeema

CHAPTER ONE

Moving beyond back to normal

If there is one singular message we have learned from the events surrounding the coronavirus pandemic that started in 2020, it's that we live in a global village and today, more than ever, the ramifications of disease, conflict and technology breakthroughs in one part of the world reverberate on the other side in equal measures of speed and impact. Innovation and transformation are two of the most hyped words in recent years and for many of us 'change' is something we want and aspire to. However, many of us also struggle with change as we may want to feel more in control, or we may feel we don't have the mechanisms to manage the upheavals around us. When change is done to us, we struggle, primarily because we lose our sense of control and we work very hard to ensure we stay in control. Or at least that's what we tell ourselves. Take, for example, recent events: since the coronavirus pandemic hit the world in 2020, we have witnessed the impact of this deadly disease across the globe, with millions losing their lives. The fallout of the disease is a global economic slowdown, leading to millions more people losing their livelihoods, their lives and the lives of their families and friends. The pandemic hit us at the same time as global warming became more prevalent and the intensification of artificial intelligence (AI) in every aspect of our lives. The culmination of these forces reminds us, in case we had forgotten, that change is constant, enormous, like a tsunami, causing unexpected and irreparable disruption.

In this time of immense change most of us will find ourselves at a crossroads; we start steering ourselves to become part of the change or we fall victim as we watch situations unfold passively. Becoming part of the change agenda means we need to consider how to navigate a route that enables us to lead, learn and build our careers better. The previous focus in this area tried, incorrectly, to focus on jobs for the future, but this approach missed the point that we are in such a state of flux, we still are unsure about what new careers will emerge over the next decade. What we do know, however, is that there are certain skills, encompassing attitudes and knowledge, that will prepare individuals to navigate the immense uncertainty in the world of work. Paul Donovan, Chief Economist for UBS Global Wealth Management explains the profound impact of this change and consequences of inaction: 'The complexity of these changes make them difficult to comprehend, and the risk is that people will be seduced by the apparent simplicity of scapegoat economics and prejudice. But this prejudice will undermine the most essential component of the fourth industrial revolution – people. It is not technology that leads economic success, but how the technology is applied. That requires the right person in the right job at the right time. Companies and countries that minimize prejudice are most likely to achieve economic success. Without inclusion, the wrong people will be employed, reducing productivity.

Without diversity, a monoculture of ideas may mean missing obvious opportunities and (more troubling) risks in a period of rapid change.'

Are you emerging out of the early blocks of your career, where you have a fairly good idea of where you want to get to, but trying to figure out how to get there? Do you feel you have knowledge just about the situation in your field but things are changing faster than you can adapt? Are you excited about the opportunities the fourth industrial revolution offers but not entirely sure what this means for you and your team? If you've answered yes (or even a slight nod) to any of these questions, keep reading – it will be worth it! If you are a little more experienced as a leader, with multiple departments and teams under your stewardship, this book is essential for you to help you support upcoming talent in the new career frontiers they will need to navigate. How will you use your experience and insights to create opportunities for your teams?

This book is designed in two parts: in the first section, we map out the impact of frontier technologies on careers and the workplace as we discuss some of the key issues that are still being tackled. We use the term 'frontier technologies' as described by the United Nations (UN), where they say, 'there is no universally agreed definition of frontier technology'. However, there is a recurring common feature across the different technological advances in that they all 'have the potential to disrupt the status quo, alter the way people live and work, rearrange value pools, and lead to entirely new products and services'. We mean such technologies to include artificial intelligence (AI) but also include biotech, nanotech, energy and advanced materials, to name a few.

The second section provides a toolkit covering the different elements of leadership to help you develop practical ways to build a more robust and resilient leadership style. We, the authors, bring together a wealth of experience working with ambitious leaders across different sectors, helping students consider career paths that have not yet been identified and research in emerging areas of leadership. Our combined experience of working and research provides the framework for this book and throughout the discussion we have provided perspectives and experiences from business leaders from a wide range of sectors and fields, who have a wealth of experience and are at the cutting edge of leadership and technology in bringing ideas to reality. If you want to gain clearer and deeper perspectives on how to develop your leadership capabilities, to meet the emerging technologies and identify which bridges you need to build for yourselves, your teams and organizations, then keep reading!

The pandemic taught us we love people as much as we love pizza

We learnt a great deal from our experiences of the pandemic. Around half of workers in most countries had to continue working through the virus: frontline staff working in healthcare and education, key support staff and those in the food sector, from farming to manufacturing and retail. The greatest transformation for many workers was the rapid and unprecedented move to home working during the spring of 2020. After the initial adrenaline-fuelled reaction to new working conditions, a great deal of research and commentary focused on the highs and lows of remote working. The light relief of video-conferencing dressing, etiquette and the benefits of autonomy and flexibility was balanced by the more sobering challenges of the disproportionate domestic burden on many, in particular women and parents who juggled parental responsibilities of learning from home.[1] At the other extreme, in many single-person households life was equally challenging, with intense feelings of loneliness. A team of researchers from MIT led by Professor Rebecca Saxe examined the impact of social isolation and found that after one day of total isolation, seeing people enjoying themselves together triggered the part of the brain, the substantia nigra (SN) located in the midbrain, which is linked with hunger cravings. The same experience was found with people who hadn't eaten all day and then viewed a picture of pizza or pasta. For individuals working from home, she suggested we literally craved human contact as we might crave a pizza when starving.

In terms of work, 2020 was the year when the philosophical questions about work and identity moved out of lecture theatres to become the central conversation in most teams and organizations. What we gain from work is complex – work clearly gives us more than financial stability. Today, more than ever, work is a source of social interactions and friendships. The range of working hours varies considerably depending on where you live and also the type of work you do, but to give you an idea, the highest annual working hours peak at 2,200 per annum in countries such as India, China,

---

[1]Research from the Boston Consulting Group identified in May 2020, across Europe and North America, on average women spent an extra 15 hours on domestic responsibilities compared to their male partners. (Janjuha-Jivraj, 2020).

Singapore, Thailand and Mexico; 1,400 hours in European countries such as Germany, Denmark and Norway. Lower working hours are correlated with countries with higher productivity – we will return to the debate on presenteeism and output later in this book.

The impact of technological advancements in the workplace help us to decipher these trends and the wider social issues that create tectonic shifts in the workplace. Guy Kirkwood, chief evangelist of robotic process automation (RPA) software company UiPath, describes 2020 as forever characterized by the grey swan event of COVID-19. In the investment world, a grey swan is the term used to describe a very significant event that is unlikely but could still happen. Its impact would potentially shake up the global economy and stock market. He explains: 'The world knew that a global pandemic was coming, we just didn't know when it would arrive. What we in the technology market did not expect is that Covid led to acceleration (not deceleration) in companies' and governments' digital transformation initiatives.'

Satya Nadella, CEO of Microsoft, described the pace of change to colleagues at Microsoft in April 2020: 'We've seen two years' worth of digital transformation in two months. From remote teamwork and learning, to sales and customer service, to critical cloud infrastructure and security – we are working alongside customers every day to help them adapt and stay open for business in a world of remote everything.[2] The world of remote everything

---

[2] www.microsoft.com/en-us/microsoft-365/blog/2020/04/30/2-years-digital-transformation-2-months/

seems inspiring, but also meaningless when it is so vast it is literally impossible to visualize what this means for us at an individual level. Kirkwood explains the three key areas that create challenges for us: 'It is the speed of change that creates the first major obstacle. The second is the availability (or lack thereof) of efficient and timely education to upskill and reskill employees and the third is the relatively poor state of employee engagement, as organizations have been focusing so much of their efforts in the past few years on customer experience.'

Essentially, all leaders need to understand how to motivate their colleagues to achieve the best outcomes for the organization. Simple enough, but what do we mean by the best outcomes? It's no longer enough to focus solely on financial measures, instead other areas become intertwined with goals and we are witnessing a notable rise in *mission-led* businesses with purposeful leadership at the core of the organization. James Uffindell, founder and CEO of Bright Network, a high-growth technology platform for graduates, is seeing a significant shift in leadership: 'For all leaders, the most important thing is vision and purpose – followers want to understandably know where we are going, why are we going there and how are we going to get there. Leaders need to work continually to hone their communication skills to articulate their vision in a way that empowers and unleashes their teams to fulfil an organization's potential.'

In these organizations we see drivers for social change are aligned with financial growth. The momentum in this area has been propelled by the UN Sustainable Development Goals (UNSDGs): https://sdgs.un.org/goals. The goals cover every element of economic and social change from climate to peace, inequality to economic growth. Unlike previous CSR-based initiatives, the UNSDGs have created an ecosystem drawing together government policy, corporate investment and civil society action to introduce and sustain behavioural change across the key areas set by the UN. As Dagmar Schumacher, Director of the Brussels office of the United Nations Development Fund for Women (UNIFEM) explains: 'In order to achieve the 2030 Agenda for Sustainable Development and the corresponding Sustainable Development Goals, financing is needed that goes far beyond the current levels of Official Development Assistance (ODA). While leveraging ODA, a sound multistakeholder approach is needed, including private sector and philanthropic investments, innovative financing as well as increased level domestic resource mobilization. The UNSDGs are creating an ecosystem to bring about sustained attitudinal and behavioural change across all sectors.'

We will come back to the notion of leadership later in the book but what we are observing is a departure in traditional approaches to leadership towards a more active approach where leadership is shared across teams and is more about doing and action, rather than titles and labels. If we consider the catalytic effect of the UNSDGs along with the impact of coronavirus, global climate change and social movements like Black Lives Matter, we see a rise in leaders openly wanting to do more for the world and for communities that are around and within their organizations. The rise of mission-led businesses focusing on social and financial performance is the result of activism permeating through civil society; non-governmental bodies keen to activate change organizations and how we work. Governance bodies in different countries are building frameworks around key social issues in the first instance to demonstrate what good practice looks like and to fuel constructive conversations – for example, the Environmental Social Governance (ESG) practices with an emphasis on green technology sets standards for operations in companies to help socially conscious investors screen potential investments. Shareholder activism is gaining momentum as a driver of change across different areas. The ESG example above demonstrates guiding principles for a more proactive and conscious approach to investment in the United Kingdom to the position adopted by Legal & General, an insurance firm with investments in every FTSE 100 company, which has issued a statement of voting against companies that do not comply with the target of recruiting at least one board member from a minority ethnic background.[3] The power of shareholder activism is recognized to catalyze change and has implications for translating conversations into purposeful action across teams and the wider workplace.

Leaders today deal with a greater complexity of problems than at any other time in history; these 'wicked problems' described by Professors W.J. Horst Rittel and Melvin M. Webber (University of California at Berkeley, 1973).[4] Wicked problems are nothing to do with good or evil but instead

---

[3]https://www.bloomberg.com/news/articles/2020-10-05/l-g-to-vote-against-company-boards-that-lack-racial-diversity

[4]Rittel, H.W.J. & Webber, M.M. (1973) 'Dilemmas in a general theory of planning'. *Policy Sci* 4, 155–169. https://doi.org/10.1007/BF01405730

describe problems with multiple complex causes and so are unlikely to have a single, simple solution, and in fact traditional solutions may create further unintended consequences and further problems.[5] This increased complexity requires leaders to grapple with big themes, leading teams where the main objective is success measured by market share, financial growth and revenue. As this discussion has identified, there will be new measures of success for companies and some of these elements may be new and difficult for organizations to incorporate.

In this book, when we discuss leadership our perspective is built on the model of distributed leadership across organizations, where leadership is the result of behaviour and attitudes rather than being specifically linked to formal appointments and titles. Leadership is not linked specifically to seniority or length of time in a certain role, there is an overwhelming source of material that will provide definitions and discussions on what constitutes leadership and we will discuss this further in Chapter 4. For the purposes of this book our position is clear: as a leader, you are committed to developing leadership skills and capabilities for your career. You may be an experienced senior leader for a team or department who is interested in understanding the perspectives of your team, particularly more junior colleagues who are demonstrating leadership qualities. The chapters in the second part of this book provide an in-depth discussion about the different aspects of leadership and consider what happens when things don't go as planned.

---

[5] https://hbr.org/2008/05/strategy-as-a-wicked-problem

Leadership turbulence and lack of consistent results provides the opportunity to learn leadership with a greater focus on agility, building resilience and transformation, and preparing for the next normal. In Chapter 2, we will discuss the 'next normal' as a way to understand the constant level of flux and how we become more comfortable being part of change. As we become more familiar with anticipating and responding to change, we adapt so fast that the past becomes another country. Throughout our lifetime, we continuously experience change, however as creatures of routine we are incredibly efficient in habituating to the change efficiently and effectively. In a sense, experiencing change is like when you are on holiday by the beach and decide to enter the sea for your first swim. When you enter the water initially the freezing-cold water feels like a bit of a shock and your instinct is to recoil, possibly even run out of the sea. But, the longer you stay and immerse yourself in the water, moving around, you eventually get used to the temperature. In other words, you habituate to the sensation and temperature and eventually, you even start to enjoy the experience. However, the impact of change has meant many of us have been dragged into the sea and experienced a sudden and powerful wave of change rather than a slow turning of the tide.

Each of you will have a different response to the initial shock and how you habituate to change. How you respond to the analogy about entering the sea will help you consider how you react to change, whether you choose it or it is imposed on you. Every age introduces innovations and new developments and more recently, the changes happen at a faster rate. The changes introduce new shocks; every new stage of work is progression, bringing greater complexity and adjustments. You have the opportunity to consider how you adapt to each phase and what you decide to habituate.

As a species that has successfully navigated biological evolution, we have developed methods of survival and the key to our success is being able to store and communicate learned behaviour across generations. The rate of change facing us means we have to update our skills and change orientation multiple times in our lifetime, which means being open to learning as we grow older. We can't assume all our learning happens in a single formalized chunk and then we tag on new skills acquisition in a passive reactive mode. Instead we need to navigate a new career path; we need to have a sense of where we are heading and ensure we are equipped with the appropriate technical and cognitive skills.

Adapting is an evolutionary response and failure to evolve leads to eventual extinction. We have all the abilities, as the most successful species, and without being too dire, as we haven't all died out (thus far). Our strength comes from our hugely successful track record in efficiency and effectiveness in responding to changes; we are extraordinarily good at evolution – if we weren't able to do this, we would be extinct.

Here is the really serious part that we want to emphasize: leadership for the next age or in the next normal is not simply avoiding complacency or redundancy, but a way to thrive and prosper – for yourself, your community, your organization and also wider society on our planet. Before we fast-forward to what the future holds, let's just remind ourselves that the world of work has undergone radical changes, impacting society, and in fact many of the discussions we are having in this book are not completely new but are ideas around change rehashed in a new environment.

The history of work – in an acorn shell

As we have said, at all stages of evolution in human society, change is a constant. To understand this, we don't need to go all the way back to Neanderthal society, we can just go through what we might think of as a recognizable work society to draw comparisons. History shows us that it was around the eighteenth century when committed office buildings became common across the world. When we talk about working from home, Professor Hannah Barker describes this as 'less of a turning point perhaps, more of a return to the older ways of doing things'.[6] In other words, returning to the first principles about work as something you do – in fact, the concept of work as a place you go – is a relatively recent phenomenon and has confused the discussion around the purpose of work.

The impact of emerging technologies is the key focus on changing working in this book, the discussion in this area shaped by experiences of previous generations. In fact, this change is called the 'Fourth Industrial Revolution' by

---

[6]Barker, H. (2020) https://www.thebritishacademy.ac.uk/blog/what-can-our-ancestors-teach-us-about-working-home/

Klaus Schwab, Founder and Executive Chairman of the World Economic Forum, drawing parallel with the previous three industrial revolutions to help us understand the scale and scope of change we are facing. Each of the previous industrial revolutions emerged as a result of breakthroughs in technology:

- First industrial revolution: mechanization of production through water and steam;
- Second industrial revolution: mass production through electricity;
- Third industrial revolution – or the introduction of electronics and information leading to automation production;
- The fourth industrial revolution we are currently experiencing builds on the third revolution but is distinct due to the rate of change and scope of impact on every aspect of our lives.

While the velocity and impact is unprecedented in the fourth industrial revolution, we can draw on learnings and experiences from the previous industrial revolutions, which provides a sense of comfort by reminding us of our ability to thrive during periods of change and turbulence. If we consider, for example, the impact of the first industrial revolution, this level of change was unprecedented. Although the Industrial Revolution had its inception in the United Kingdom in the eighteenth century, it spread throughout the world, influencing working patterns and societies.

The impact of change created enormous economic and social transformation; the rise of factories and machines led to standardized production, allowing customers to purchase cheaper goods. Innovations of mass production such as the spinning jenny (which revolutionized textile manufacturing), created more efficiencies in workplaces and international trading routes in turn established foreign markets and investment in transport infrastructures. Further along the supply chain, factories increased energy consumption, transport demands increased for distributing goods, escalating fossil fuel consumption. Producers accumulated wealth and additional taxes on goods and trade generated further sources of income for governments. Alongside manufacturing growth, the Industrial Revolution saw huge advances in medicine and renewed interest in science and technological innovations. This period of intense activity created the foundations for modern capitalism as the world witnessed unprecedented growth in consumption and production. Alongside the growth in markets was the expansion in social movements, coalescing around workers' rights, along with environmental and social concerns. Working patterns institutionalized in our lives today emerged from this period, including the idea of a weekend, unions and the inception of equality movements on pay and working conditions.

The migration of workers from agriculture into factories not only meant a boom in urbanization (paving the way for the megacities we see today), but it also created jobs as we experience them in the twenty-first century. As factory workers gained more skills and technological innovation flooded workplaces, professions became more specialized. Apprenticeships flourished, creating clusters of highly skilled workers who could create repeat tasks. The growth of demand for products increased the requirements for skilled work. Many of the skills that emerged during this period were still valued during the subsequent second and third industrial revolutions.

Leadership as a function focused on improving efficiencies through productivity, and research from the early 1900s focused on creating conditions to maximize output. The dominant thinking in leadership during this time emerged from the great man theory, where by the Scottish historian and essayist Thomas Carlyle (1795–1881) incited hero worship of this model of leadership.[7] Carlyle was a sharp observer of industrial change and wrote about its impact, as well as the perceptions of leadership. This view argued that leaders, who at that time were predominantly men, were born with the traits and characteristics necessary for leadership. The leadership style described as commanding, direct and impersonal was also replicated across factories and organizations dealing with the delivery of production and services. Over the last 50 years, the range of leadership models and frameworks has evolved in alignment with changes in social trends and industry shifts, but in many cases the foundations of thinking have emerged from research on previous groups; often white, middle-class male companies focusing on mass outputs of production or services.

As leaders extend beyond this homogenous group to include women and wider socio-economic and ethnic backgrounds, the evidence base for leadership has

[7]Carlyle, T. (1841) *On Heroes, Hero-Worship, and the Heroic in History*. London, James Fraser.

broadened and new models need to take into account this diversity of experience. Since 2000, the field of leadership education has witnessed an explosion of leadership models and frameworks with a wider base of behaviours, including vulnerability, storytelling, empathy and diversity, as well as concepts of psychological safety, teaming, growth mindset and career resilience (we will discuss these in Chapter 10 as part of your toolkit). The twentieth century witnessed the permanency of careers; a job for life became the mantra upon the completion of formal education. In the twenty-first century, however, we see life-long careers evaporate and career volatility is now commonplace. Leadership practices have had to adapt to handle this level of uncertainty, particularly when changes need to happen rapidly. In the next chapter we will examine what the next normal means and how this impacts our understanding of work.

CHAPTER TWO

Adapting to the next normal

You will recognize by now the central theme to this book is being prepared for change and this is why we have consciously chosen to call this chapter 'the next normal' rather than 'the new normal'. During the pandemic of 2020 and beyond, commentators and researchers invested sizeable amounts of time and words predicting what our new reality would look like. The new normal assumes the next phase of a change as a one-off event that will create change, which then becomes cemented in the foreseeable future. In a conversation with Zabeen Hirji, former Chief Human Resources Officer of the Royal Bank of Canada and currently advisor to a range of sectors, Executive Advisor for the Future of Work at Deloitte and Executive-in-residence Beedie School of Business at Simon Fraser University, Canada, we discussed the difference in perspectives between 'new normal' and 'next normal'. Hirji argues the term normal, 'creates a premature approach to understanding change because we still don't understand what the change means for us. We are committing to an abstract notion of change without a clear articulation of what this means for us. In essence, we need to get comfortable with the next normal because we have to get used to being in an ever-changing environment.'

Whether or not we realize it, we have been adapting to changes in the workplace perhaps since we were first asked that magical question, 'What do you want to do when you grow up?' Can you remember the first time you were asked that question? More importantly, do you recall how the question was asked? Was it, 'What do you want to be when you grow up?' or 'What do you want to do when you grow up?' and perhaps these questions became a recurrent theme for you. If you were lucky, maybe the questions evolved into 'What impact do you want to make on the world?' Why does this last question matter? Well, the first questions focus on jobs shaped by what we already know exists in the world. Your impact is not limited by a job or role – in fact, you may have to create a role to achieve the impact you expect to make. If this sounds too good to be true, we've come across some fantastic people who have done just that in carving out roles for themselves in Chapter 10 (*see also* pp. 195–213).

Research points to the importance of our formative experiences shaping our career ambitions and expectations – for example, research on girls' attitudes towards science, technology, engineering and mathematics (STEM) subjects show the considerable influence of careers' attitudes towards gender influencing the role play of younger boys and girls. Being able to engage with role models and mentors who are not only inspirational but also accessible makes all the difference in broadening the range of career horizons for children. Playing by the rules is a route that has been successful for generations through education and careers but the reality is the rules have changed so much. The rules that existed when we made these decisions no longer exist and the decisions that need to be made can be quite overwhelming.

Coming back to that question, the chances are you answered in a very practical way, providing a specific solution to a problem or grabbing an opportunity. Leadership is not a common response to early role play but the balanced combination of personality and experiences creates the foundation of leading others and getting feedback on what it means to make decisions. As you transition through different stages of education and embark on your career, there is an implicit assumption that progression means taking on more responsibility and accountability, honing your leadership skills to manage larger groups of people achieving even greater productivity. This approach works on the assumption that careers are linear and correlated to age and length of time working in a specific role. However, over the last decade the workplace has become a giant experiment, lab-trialling new approaches to working – for example, flexible working, gig working, four-day working weeks, hybrid working and equally new approaches to interpersonal relationships; reverse mentoring, board mentoring programmes, apprenticeship opportunities across all sectors. Naeema's research specifically found that work is increasingly non-linear, while company career development structures assume career linearity (Pasha, 2020).[8] The range of initiatives in the workplace flourished under the

---

[8]https://adventuresincareerdevelopment.wordpress.com/2020/04/14/issue-44-of-the-nicec-journal-now-out/

diversity agenda to create working conditions that are more inclusive and accommodating for a more diverse workforce. The impact of the lockdown as a result of the coronavirus forced some of these areas to become modus operandi for organizations, particularly in countries resistant to this level of change. Karina Govindji, who works as EMEA Director of Diversity, Equity & Inclusion for Google, explains the impact: 'Covid has fast-tracked flexible working in a way that no one thought was possible. Cultures like India, where presenteeism has been so important – if I don't see you, you are not working – have had to move to this way of working, which would have taken several decades for culture shift to happen.' India represents challenges faced by countries dominated by traditional approaches to working; despite the growing trend of high-tech and financial services firms, the majority of its workforce is still employed in retail and agriculture sectors that are dominated by onsite production. The impact of the hybrid model over 2020 means the experimentation is now taking root and Govindji goes on to explain the impact: 'It's hard to imagine work life ever being the same again, with five days a week in offices and extensive travel to other countries.'

It is now standard practice for most organizations to have four generations working together (Boomers, Gen X, Millennials and Gen Z). Ignoring the politics of labels for different age groups, the pressure is to create workplace cultures that allow the different groups to feel comfortable and create a sense of belonging. One of the most transformational experiences of COVID-19 is the shift from tinkering with new ways of working to a commitment to new ways of working. Sathya Bala, Head of Global Data Governance at a luxury goods company, identifies the opportunities facing organizations: 'If businesses take the approach to go back to normal or back to the way things were [that] would be disappointing and a huge wasted opportunity. There are things we have learnt as individuals, teams and companies. We should take the good bits, the creativity that comes from disruption and reset who we want to be at work, how we want to work and what our culture should be. In a crisis we tend to work more effectively. Of course we do not want more crises, but we need to keep some of that creative problem solving that happened when we had to quickly change our ways of working. There was a sense of coming together to tackle a problem without a fear of failure and without firmly drawn lines of what sits in someone's role or not.'

Furthermore, social movements and exponential climate change impacts every aspect of society. For all future and current leaders, futureproofing leadership comes with understanding not only that times change, but so too does leadership and as such, so do leadership skills and mindsets.

The greatest step to leadership

In Chapter 1, we introduced our perspective on leadership beyond the titles and accolades and focusing on the activity and impact of leadership behaviour and also how the nature of leadership research has evolved over the decades. The leadership giants of the American Dream from the mass-market age (1950s–90s) often occupied the persona of the heroic hero, the super-hero type of leaders – people such as Jack Welch, CEO of GE, a global icon renowned for his motivational sermons in 'The Pit' (which was a designed space within a pitched arena) to leaders of other great US corporations. His style was a defining approach to success, creating an almost mythological attitude to leadership; his approach as tough-talking and singularly focused on shareholder value yielded results in the market-driven growth of the enterprise culture economy dominating the US. To achieve success, he regularly assessed staff, removing the 10 per cent who didn't make the cut; his corporate advantage was based on company acquisition to grow market share and with equal efficiency divesting companies (and staff) that were a drain. He was critical of organizations he felt were too paternalistic in their culture towards staff.

While this leadership style still exists in many companies, the turbulence in the business environment has created space for different cultures to emerge and demonstrate corporate success. Take, for example, IBM, which is comparable to GE in terms of scale and size. The founding principles expressed by Thomas J. Watson are still at the heart of the American multinational: 'The trouble with every one of us is that we don't think enough. We don't get paid for working with our feet – we get paid for working with our heads.' The founding principles: respect for the individual, employee participation, encouragement of 'thoughtful risks in management decision making', being a good place to work. The impact of IBM in the computer field is commonplace: producing the world's first mass-produced computer in 1951 and selling 10,000 units with products used in 79 countries.

Perhaps less well known is its impact on society – IBM hired its first disabled worker in 1941, appointing its first female vice-presidents in 1943 and first black sales rep three years later. Speaking to Deborah Richards, who is the former UKI Diversity & Inclusion Lead for IBM for the UK and Ireland, she explains how the founding principles underpin the organization's reaction to COVID-19: 'I think that everyone has to be able to connect and manage, and collaborate, both with their own teams but also with clients, virtually. Everyone is having to work in a completely different way. Technology is fundamentally going to change the way we work. All sorts of roles that traditionally would have been clerical or back office are now done by systems and chatbots. And it means the skill level has to evolve and change.'

Successful leadership is contingent on proactive thinking, identifying trends and acting quickly and decisively. This is the most challenging aspect of leadership, either because individuals feel they don't have sufficient experience to make an informed decision or they are so comfortable, they become complacent. The impact of the pandemic has demonstrated leadership at its best and worst; the rise of a new wave of political (predominantly female) leadership with a balance between science and empathy challenging the strongman leadership embodied by former US President Donald Trump. The spectacular collapse of businesses – for example, Arcadia, the global retail brand led by Philip Green, who was annihilated in a governmental report on the pensions scandal in 2016 for his lack of ethics and avarice: 'What kind of man is it who can count his fortune in billions but does not know what decent behaviour is?' stated Frank

Field, Chair of the UK Work and Pensions committee.[9] In 2000, GE was valued at $600 billion and while people may say valuations are always a little fantastical, the fact is its valuation was at $60 billion as of December 2020.

As leaders become caught up in their narrative of success there is a tendency to fall victim to self-serving bias; you know, the one where people credit themselves for success but will place blame for failure on others or extraneous circumstances. This specific behaviour makes it even more difficult for a leader to adapt and continuously manage uncertainty well. The modern status of CEO makes them into celebrities like A-list Hollywood stars. Mythologizing the abilities of a CEO without critical thinking creates a bubble of assumption that they know everything and omnipotent. However, many leaders, particularly entrepreneurs, fuel this leadership, which is deeply charismatic but also controlling.

The year 2020 was a fascinating year for observing the sliding scales of leadership. Sometimes events come so far out of leftfield that will impact a company, there is no way they could have anticipated it and the subsequent impact is not due to the leader at that time. Events such as the Great Financial Crash of 2008 caused companies such as GE to lose liquidity and assets. Leadership reactions to the global COVID-19 pandemic has led to immense losses or gains even within the same sectors; consider the entertainment industry – the losses experienced by the entertainment sector where (pre-COVID) almost half of their revenue

---

[9]https://publications.parliament.uk/pa/cm201617/cmselect/cmworpen/54/5402. htm?utm_source=54&utm_medium=fullbullet&utm_campaign=modulereports

relied on theatre/cinema releases compared to the 21 per cent growth of Netflix revenue in 2020.[10]

It is therefore critical to have the foresight to look beyond the everyday to understand the trends, what infrastructures need to be developed *and how to influence others to listen and act.* The pandemic demonstrates more clearly than anything that nothing stays the same and some organizations will fail. The willingness to recognize this provides leaders with the edge needed to not get too comfortable. Consider what Jeff Bezos predicted in 2018: 'Amazon is not too big to fail. In fact, I predict one day, Amazon will fail. Amazon will go bankrupt. If you look at large companies, their lifespans tend to be 30-plus years, not 100-plus years.' This prediction, shared by CNBC in a recording of Bezos speaking to his staff, identifies the ability to get beyond the comfort zone and figure out what is ahead of us.[11]

We don't have a crystal ball and we can't predict the future. We can see the general trends, but how do we distil this information and understand specifically what this means for each of us? Consider a big theme in this book: frontier technology. Every organization is operating in this climate even if they may not realize the degree to which this is happening. We will discuss this later on. Organizations have concerns about terrorism and security as well as the impact of huge climate change. The generalized nature of these concerns means they are huge, complex and overwhelming. At the

---

[10]https://www.statista.com/chart/21465/global-paid-net-subscriber-additions-by-net-flix/

[11]https://www.cnbc.com/2018/11/15/bezos-tells-employees-one-day-amazon-will-fail-and-to-stay-hungry.html

same time, global companies compete in tighter markets, while they see a rise in population and a fall in productivity.

How do emerging leaders manage such external complexities, as well as develop their teams and themselves? We will discuss this in more detail, but we feel one way to start for all leaders is to seek or reaffirm what your career purpose is; establish what affirms you and what resources you have to manage change, which may also include how you challenge structures effectively; consider whether you think ethically and how you understand the impact of your decisions on the people, the organization and the planet. Remember that question we discussed at the beginning of this chapter: 'What impact do you want to make?' There has never been a better opportunity to reflect on your career and consciously consider how you map out your career. Being prepared for change requires a shift in mindset, as described by Laurie Paxton, Chief People Officer of Sitalia: 'Success is not static, nor should our qualities, skills and mindsets be fixed. From a mindset perspective, it should be about questioning what we think we know. Solutions should always be evolving and therefore we should always be questioning them.'

To focus in on your impact, let's get specific about the impact of artificial intelligence (AI) and through this discussion start the journey of understanding of how it will influence you as a leader and, more excitingly, how you can shape the future of work.

Managing an AI tsunami

As a leader you will need a strong view and clear perspective on AI; you won't have all the answers, but you will need to understand when AI will impact your individual career path. Not if, or how, but when. Neeti Shukla, co-founder of the American company, Automation Anywhere, shares her perspectives on emerging technology: 'As with many innovations that are the result of some life-altering moments in technology, in this case, RPA and AI – both together and separately – serve as catalysts for the future of work. We will see in the next five to 10 years, these technologies become even more mainstream – unleashing new possibilities for services, new and improved product development, and ultimately, new and improved ways for businesses to serve their customers.'

Currently, we know AI and automation is impacting jobs, not in a small, incremental way, but by wiping out swathes of roles. Predictions of AI and the workplace focus on specific trends – for example, in October 2020 the World Economic Forum (WEF) produced a major report on the Future of Jobs. The report highlighted that the rise of AI machines and automation would eliminate 85 million jobs by 2025. Furthermore, many more millions of jobs will adapt to using AI. However, the WEF also says that while this statistic looks startling, they suggest that the world economy will adapt to create new jobs. Similar to previous industrial revolutions, new jobs will arise in areas we may not be able to predict. In fact, WEF expects 97 million new jobs to be created, which means an overall addition of 12 million.[12]

Where will these new jobs come from? Some will be from applying new forms of frontier technologies, such as AI,

---

[12]https://www.weforum.org/reports/the-future-of-jobs-report-2020

but also in, say, nanotech (nanotechnology is a specialist technology building applications at the size of atoms and molecules, and it's suggested that nanotech could have enormous impact on a range of industries, including human health). WEF also suggests that jobs will grow in emerging green tech as the world tries to meet challenges in climate. These could include vertical agriculture and shifts in renewable energy technology uses. All commentators and the co-authors will emphasize that with the huge changes ahead, the need for 'reskilling' and 'upskilling' has never been greater: for you as leaders adapting your skills, but also in a wider context – there is a critical need for leaders to ensure staff are sufficiently equipped for the future of work. Let's pick a well-known example: the impact of autonomous vehicles and in particular, driverless trucks. The immediate impact will be swathes of drivers losing their jobs; initial estimates predict 2–3 million trucking jobs will disappear as a result of automation. We also know that the pipeline for truck drivers isn't that strong, so alternatives need to be found. We believe that while the risk of job loss from automation is very real, the projections that often get touted are overstated in some job areas (truck drivers, data input clerks, accountants and bookkeepers are all being watched by the bots). Anyway, let's return to the philosophy of jobs. The rise of autonomous vehicles, it is said, will push out most truck drivers. If we unpack some of this argument, if we assume we find a neat route to switching to AI autonomous vehicles, which would necessitate a new transportation infrastructure that includes fuelling, what then do we do with truck drivers? In our discussion in Chapter 1 on previous industrial revolutions (*see also* pp. 22–25), we discussed how we handled obsolete jobs by retraining people in new areas of opportunity. A challenge we face in the fourth industrial revolution suggests that new job creation may not happen simultaneously, at least according to commentators such as Daniel Susskind, Fellow in Economics at Balliol College, Oxford, an author whose studies on the future of work examines what a world without work will mean for our sense of identity and purpose. Susskind argues that new jobs will emerge but not in the numbers to meet current rates of population increase and that we also face an asymmetry in the type of jobs required and the skills available to do them. He also says it's not just the truck drivers who will be displaced by AI and automation, but all jobs, such as medical doctors and lawyers. Many other commentators do not agree, among them Paul Donovan, Chief Economist at UBS, who suggests that this revolution will create enough new jobs – a view adopted by WEF in their analysis.

If we think again about our truck drivers, in principle there is nothing to stop them being retrained as coders, programmers or data scientists. A small proportion of drivers will grab the opportunity to retrain (more on this in Chapter 9), but others won't because of factors such as not seeing value in changing, the amount retraining might cost, worrying about retraining and concerns over their identity, or a range of understandable concerns and resistance to retraining. A few will retrain, but others won't, yet all our truck drivers still need to feed themselves and their families and, we assume, want to be busy.

The likely impact of AI on jobs is more fragmented and complex than this example suggests. David Autor, Professor of Economics at MIT, states, 'We could manage this incoming change, you as leaders can manage this. Our premise is that while we all know change is a constant, we as humans also seek out continuity (it drives our human safety needs). In many ways, we inherently don't like change because we are creatures of habit. We are also change-adverse, because we're so efficient at the systems of today, we don't make changes we need for tomorrow, because it requires additional energy to be used. If we think about our truck drivers, in principle, there is nothing to stop them being retrained as coders or programmers, but in honesty, we can't make such sweeping changes – but we can consider how we manage change in incremental shifts.'

Autor argues in his paper, 'Why Are There Still So Many Jobs?'[13] that the future of AI and automation will not remove jobs at many levels as AI is not skilled enough to take them on, saying, 'My own prediction is that employment polarization will not continue indefinitely. While some of the tasks in many current middle-skill jobs are susceptible to automation, many middle-skill jobs will continue to demand a mixture of tasks from across the skill spectrum.' He goes on to say that many lower-skilled jobs will also survive and it is more likely that mundane and repetitive work can and will be automated. Even then, that might only apply to some parts of some people's jobs. He does warn us, however, that

---

[13]https://economics.mit.edu/files/11563

skilling is essential for workers to develop resilience in the job market – something we discuss further in Chapter 9.

The entrepreneur and philanthropist (and one-time US presidential candidate) Andrew Yang has proposed that if we are unable to retrain people, a universal basic income (UBI) is needed – a kind of monetary benefit paid by the government, by taxing AI companies. What, then, will our truck driver community do? There are many people who say they will be free to run through meadows, play the violin or following other creative pursuits as they no longer work gruelling hours and for a faceless, uncaring capitalist company. Interestingly, creative roles are far less susceptible to the impact of AI.

We feel that the new economy will probably adjust and employment will remain full (or near-full), but there will be a lot of adaptation and adjustment within jobs as AI enters most roles and yes, some job areas will disappear (as in all industrial revolutions) and so our truck drivers will need to find new work. In this debate, we need to remember that fundamentally, as a race, we thrive when we work. We like work, even though sometimes we don't like Mondays. But we like work as a place for social interaction, wealth creation and sharing, giving us a sense of self-worth and deep value. Often our identity is tied up in our work and we take pride in sharing it, our contribution to our professions and our cause. Remember the story (which may be an urban myth, but the essence is right) that is now enshrined in purposeful leadership: in 1962, when US President John F. Kennedy made his first visit to NASA, he apparently met a janitor carrying a broom. When the President asked what he did, the janitor replied, 'I'm helping to put a man on the moon.' In the same vein, we need to remember that truck drivers are the backbone of modern living and without them, we would not have the life we enjoy. Let's not minimize the value of work to ourselves and the value of workers to society.

In order to protect what we value, we need to recognize that we have control. At a macro level, when we talk about change it becomes overwhelming and anxiety-inducing because we feel out of control. Let's change the narrative position: we can manage the change and have control over how we manage the elements that have a direct impact on us. If we let change pass us by, we will get sucked into the wave. But if we pay attention to the change and the trajectory, we can adapt and respond and navigate ourselves by preparing for change before we are ambushed.

This is the crux of leadership – seeing the bigger picture, identifying what is ahead, creating a vision to navigate the change and enabling the resources to be implemented for this to happen. It's not easy – consider, for example, Microsoft co-founder Bill Gates, who in 2015 forecast the spread of a global pandemic. He had all the elements in place required to handle a global pandemic but even with his sphere of influence and recognition, it wasn't enough to mobilize resources on a worldwide scale to limit or halt the impact of coronavirus. This doesn't mean we don't do it, but it's hard work and we need to be prepared for that level of effort. The impact of coronavirus has served to hasten the pace of change shared by Neeti Shukla of Automation Anywhere: 'The pandemic changed the way most organizations conduct business and automation has played a front-and-centre role in this change. Acceleration of many trends in the business world, including digitization, became imperative for many organizations and essential to several industries. Without digitization, companies are not able to support working remotely or even serving their customers without disruption. Healthcare, government services and financial institutions experienced an even more immediate need to deliver faster to market therapeutics, vaccines and economic relief packages.'

One of the things we want to raise is that we do have control. The starting point is recognizing that change is constant. For most of our lives it has happened incrementally (like us acclimatizing to the sea). In the world of business, pandemic change aside, large-scale transformations do not occur overnight. The transformation happens incrementally and not always in a linear fashion. Consider for example the technology we use for communication and how this has changed over the last 30 years from one landline phone in a household to social media messaging on your smartphone from almost anywhere in the world to anyone in the world. It can feel like the technology is outsmarting us and that as humans we need to catch up with the full potential of these developments. The gap is knowing what technology can do and how to harness it well. The gap is reduced by leaders who have the vision, the acumen and courage to make bold decisions and take leaps forward while others speculate. We acknowledge the need for creativity and risk but also recognize appetite needs a bite-sized approach.

Richard Foster-Fletcher, CEO of NeuralPath.io, an artificial intelligence advisory and strategy practice, host of the *Boundless* podcast and MKAI Chair, explains the need for personal leadership: 'The three most in-demand employee skills in the future are likely to be: complex problem solving, critical thinking and creativity. The latter should be kept in mind for leaders that employ data-driven decision making. The art of good leadership will be to effectively leverage data assets without discouraging human-creativity.'

For many people being a hero is synonymous with being a leader (remember, what impact do you want to make?). As leaders, responding to swathes of change can be achieved by nudging. The concept of nudging, devised by Nobel prize-winner Richard Thaler, is adopted by behavioural economists, where by subtle policy shifts encourage people to act in a way that is in their best interests – without imposing penalties for non-adherence: 'By knowing how people think, we can make it easier for them to choose what is best for them, their families and society.' If we think about applying the nudge effect in the workplace, it has huge benefits for promoting the reskilling agenda and reframing our approach to AI.

Nudging behaviour is really important for leaders to consider when it comes to bringing about effective change since it enables us to consider the impacts and influences of new stuff. There's the sense that AI is more like a tsunami that will just sweep us up and we are powerless to resist. Some might try but they may get sucked back into the water. Others, the individuals who are the super-skilled, might say they will find their way to get to the highest building and likely survive. But, what if we are fighting against the wrong image? If we recognize that this mental picture that has been presented to us is rooted in fear, whereas it's actually about us having the ability to shape shift? So, instead of a tsunami image associated with AI, we shift to a slower water image of smaller waves, where we can visualize a change that we can manage. We become less fearful, because the change is broken down and is less overwhelming.

If we say rather than creating a tsunami, we are creating ripples of smaller, continuous change, then the anxiety subsides and ripples allow for that incremental change. So, yes, at some point, millions of people will lose their jobs, but it won't be a sudden large-scale shutdown and the pre-warning enables opportunities to nudge drivers into new jobs armed with the appropriate skills. We are going to get rid of our millions of truck drivers, at some point that will happen, but it doesn't have to be this large-scale shutdown shift and we can find ways to ensure all workers find meaning and value – ideally in jobs. We still want to keep the fabric of society and what makes us human and allows us to stay in work. A new future of work, sure, but still work.

CHAPTER THREE

AI – what every leader needs to understand

In Chapter 2, we introduced the impact of AI on our working lives. It's hard to overstate the impact of disruption we will experience across every element of our lives. Of course the challenge for us to fully comprehend this is the shift from an abstract concept to the reality of what this looks and feels like. As we discussed earlier, the pace of technology development is moving at such a fast rate that by the time the change is made in our workplaces we will have already missed the opportunity to help shape that impact. One of the biggest challenges in this area is the chasm between the technology experts and non-tech leaders.

Ann Cairns, Executive Vice Chair at MasterCard, explains the opportunity and the challenge: 'We are seeing huge leaps in technology, 5G [5G is the fifth generation technology standard for broadband cellular networks, and the planned successor to the 4G networks that provide connectivity to most current cellphones] and advances through quantum computing. [This has happened in] a very short number of years, and that is going to change the whole way that artificial intelligence works. And so we're going to have an amazing opportunity to revamp the whole way that we work, how we augment ourselves with machines. You don't have to be someone who is a technology 'expert' to use and benefit from technology. So, people, and women in particular, have to stop being disinterested in it.

'I mean, I'm not very interested in playing complex games and I actually don't like coding. It wasn't my thing, I'm not that kind of techie. I'm much more motivated in understanding how to use and apply tech in our work and finding out how to make the tech easier to access and use. Global companies and the startup industry need people that are creative, and they know they need them. They probably need the skills more than they need the bog-standard programmers so actually what we need is for people to learn how to use it.'

In this chapter we are going to provide a dive into AI, a guide for non-techie readers to get to grips with the core elements of AI and how we can understand its application and impact. We also deal with one of the biggest challenges facing leaders: the ethical considerations of AI in our lives.

The history of AI in an acorn shell

AI stands for artificial intelligence. It was coined by a group of scientists in Dartmouth College, USA, in the summer of 1956, who wanted to recreate human intelligence in computers. Essentially, AI is now used as a term for a set of emerging technologies. Many of these tools and techniques focus on creating models based on rules or 'algorithms' using machine learning (ML). Much of AI development and research generally uses rule-based systems, where information is stored, accumulated and used based on a set of guidelines (the rule-based type is used in robot process automation (RPAs), as we discussed in the previous chapter, *see also* pp. 52–53). Employing statistical techniques such as regression modelling (to determine which variables in an equation have an impact on the outcome), the rules use the data to form predictions and groupings. Machine learning means that AI systems can learn from the data it is given and offer solutions, the difference being the vast amount of data and computer power and speed at which AI systems work compared to previous times, which is why we've seen the leaps in AI over this last decade.

AI use in reasoning, problem solving, perception and also language and emotion is where much of AI development is focused. Subsections of AI include deep learning, where the AI model is trained to learn on its own as it uses data that is both unstructured and unlabelled. The results are astonishing for sure, giving us 'human-like' speech, pattern and image recognition. However, let's not get too hyped. AI, while called 'intelligent', still as yet does not match any human brain. While it may read emotions, it does not have emotions. An AI game winning at chess, sadly, cannot enjoy the victory.

Before we go into the use of AI we see in our life, as well as what we will expect in the next few decades, we want to mention artificial general intelligence (AGI) – the point at which machine intelligence would take over human intelligence, creating an artificial super intelligence (ASI). Many authors see AGI as an inevitable result of the ongoing march of the machines, calling the moment this point is achieved as 'The Singularity', where technological advances are at an almost uncontrollable rate of innovation. It feels the subject of sci-fi and it's fair to say many more commentators and academics suggest this probably will not happen – and if it does, it won't be in this century! But it's nevertheless worth keeping an eye on.

However, a leap forwards in technology that is more of a possibility in a shorter timescale is quantum computing. We are seeing vast investment by computer giants such as IBM into this technology. Why are they and others doing this? The expectation is that quantum computing will provide a huge jump in computational power, to it being able to perform at a level that even current supercomputers can't do, providing the ability to address huge issues that we can't look at now – such as the detailed impact of pollution on the climate, or even working in conjunction with supercomputers to answer questions about planetary and space science. We won't go into the technology behind them, we won't even predict if and when these bigger frontier technologies will come in, but as a leader you'll need to be aware that there will always be some technology ahead of you. A leader needs to be discerning about hype and potential.

It is only in this last decade, however, that AI has taken a greater place in our world, partly driven by computational advances, but also enormous investments by large tech firms and countries. If we recognize that entertainment provides us with glimpses into AI but also separate reality and mythology, we start to spot flashes of life imitating art. In reality much of our AI interactions already exist and would make pretty dull viewing on the big or small screen. If you are reading this book on a personal device or a smartphone or you ordered it online, the chances are you engaged with AI to get here. The truth is that you are already experiencing a lot of AI technology as so much is hidden. Your smartphone operates on AI, your AI assistants like Siri and Google offer you suggestions for travel routes, recipes, jokes or whatever you need. AI that uses a range of technologies such as computer vision, natural language processing, natural language understanding, virtual and augmented reality, and robot and intelligence processing is seamlessly part of our day-to-day lives. Your music recommendations in Spotify and SoundCloud have been tracking your listening and want to give you a more personalized experience. Facebook is using AI to track malignant content, rather than letting its human monitors suffer the very real trauma of seeing harmful and abusive material. Your email will use AI to offer predictive words and sentences based on whom you are emailing, while facial recognition allows you to access your phone, laptop and banking apps.

Ahead of us are more innovations in technology with the growth of robots in workplaces, education settings and homes. The field of human-robot interaction (HRI) has seen a huge increase in recent times. The hope for HRI is that it will provide robots that have a high human interface to offer solutions not just in manufacturing (where robots have been used for decades) but also to be used as pets to alleviate loneliness as well as working in hazardous areas such as nuclear plant decommissioning, and intricate areas such as within surgery. We also see AI being used in healthcare, climate, vaccine development and cancer detection, enabling wider diagnoses through accessing complex research papers. For education, software that detects plagiarism compares high school, college and university assignments within cohorts, across cohorts and with published sources, and updates becomes sensitive to styles of writing. In the consumer marketplace, online personalized purchasing has been propelled to the next level by lockdowns and the closure of non-essential retail. It is now possible to purchase foundation to match your skin shade using facial recognition technology, and the same applies to lipstick. One thing is certain: the pandemic has completely changed the way we experience shopping in beauty halls.

Shopping aside, the deeper issues now facing AI focus on how technology interacts with humans and what frameworks will need to be in place to navigate our future. Other elements emerging include robotic process automation (RPA), which is different to AI but complements it well. RPA is the use of software bots (programs) to automate highly repetitive, routine tasks; replicating work normally carried out by knowledge workers. Examples of RPA include call centre operations supporting common queries and solutions, with RPA consolidating information before the more complex queries are passed to a human or onboarding employees, where new recruits receive necessary documentation. The next time you have an appointment with a healthcare professional, the chances are this will be set up by a bot, who has gathered your details, insurance information, appointment requests, location preferences and then provides you with appointment options. The same will happen with your next credit card application. Not only do bots gather information, but they will also carry out background checks to decide if your credit score is approved for a credit card.

These examples illustrate the ramifications of RPA for organizations: cost reduction, market differentiation. As with traditional approaches to strategic planning for businesses it's critical to be clear on the value proposition of the chosen approach and ensure the right tools are being applied. If you believe your organization needs to invest in RPAs to carry out large repetitive tasks, you may also consider the costs and benefits of deploying staff to more innovative tasks and areas that become paramount to recovery.

Let's also consider the impact of virtual reality (VR) and its more recent development, augmented reality (AR). If you're not a gamer, the chances are VR and AR may seem abstract terms that have something to do with headsets. In a word, yes, using headsets, VR provides you with an opportunity to immerse yourself in a new world – particularly useful for gaming, but increasingly important for organizations. AR in comparison allows you to still remain in the 'real world' but you can augment it while wearing smart glasses or using the camera on your phone to overlay information on your surroundings. Both VR and AR offer clear competitive advantages for businesses, although the benefit of AR or VR actually depends on how easy the solution they offer is and how quickly they can be commercialized. Ease of access is essential, both for integration in the business as well as how other stakeholders engage with the technology.

VR is being adopted by a number of businesses to enable better remote working – for example, investment bank UBS is working with Microsoft's HoloLens team trialling AR to enable traders who work from home under lockdown to have an immersive virtual reality trading floor experience. This development creates great benefit for maintaining trading during disruption to work and providing wider access, but it is still likely that many workers prefer less cumbersome work experience.

Hilton Hotels use VR to create empathetic training programmes for corporate staff to better understand the demands on operations teams when dealing with multiple complex requests from guests. Blaire Bhojwani, Hilton's Senior Director of Learning Innovation, states: 'Our goal was to make our corporate team members virtually sweat.' The direct and indirect benefits (improved service and efficient modes of training) of this cross-functional training beautifully illustrate how technology and leadership development combine to improve the experiences of employees and customers. The concept is fantastic, however there are some hurdles from a technology perspective. Despite the enormous progress with VR headsets, users still need to wear a cumbersome headset, which can be uncomfortable or look awkward in an office setting.

Augmented reality (AR) blends our world with the imagined world in a more 'real' way. It creates a way of visualizing objects that would be impossible to see otherwise. To achieve this impact, AR enables us to add virtual layers of real-time information, 3D images and movement to the world while we still remain in the physical world. It's comfortable and easier to experience and a key driver in this technology is placing the user needs at the centre of designing the solution.

As with most emerging technology, ease of use is a strong predictor of adoption for the end user. AR has significant advantages for users in terms of use through phones and augmenting reality. We only have to look at an early example, when Pokémon GO was a runaway success in summer 2016 – grossing $100 million for Nintendo in just 20 days. The take-up rate of players, who were able to access AR through their phones, was phenomenal, leading to Pokémon GO setting five world records in revenue, downloads and those magical 20 days achieved by a mobile game. The design-centred approach to Pokémon GO brought together AR and gamified tools to open this channel of gaming to a wider playing audience. The same records would not have been achieved through a VR channel.

Beyond the world of gaming, AR becomes big business. Richard Foster-Fletcher of NeuralPath.io explains the shift across the business sector for business to business (B2B), as well as the more familiar business to consumer (B2C) area: 'Augmented Reality is not just for consumer-oriented businesses, there are strong use cases in B2B industries, especially manufacturing and construction.' Consider for example Airbus using HoloLens 2 to help train production workers and give them access to contextual instructions and pertinent information. Airbus is so certain that AR technology will improve manufacturing productivity that they have partnered with Microsoft to develop an AR learning solution that they will sell as a stand-alone product across the industry.

The applications of emerging technology are endless and even more exciting as businesses become more creative with the application to different functions. The overlap between entertainment and working will increase, creating different experiences of what working means and how new ideas emerge.

Getting comfortable with frontier technology in the workplace

Where are the tech conversations in your organization? You may not be aware of them but they are happening and on a frequent basis. There is the tendency to think along the siloed lines of functions and imagine a group of AI geeks working on complex random programs that are of limited relevance to our working lives. This may well be the case in a number of organizations, but the more forward-thinking companies are engaging with technology and using it as a lens to understand how roles are morphing. Hubs and units will be working on innovation, bringing in new ways of considering functions. Deloitte's Zabeen Hirji shares her experiences of technological advancements in the banking sector:

'Banks have gone through a number of rounds of automation over the last three decades and set off on their digitization journey over 10 years ago. We can expect this to accelerate as we see AI being used across many functions. This means most routine tasks will be automated and even "knowledge" work is being automated through the use of robotics and AI. Take cyber security, for example. Machines can do what humans could never do. They are capable of analyzing massive amounts of data at breakneck speed and flag when human intervention is needed to review the data and make judgement calls.'

Selma Turki, Cognitive Solution Leader at EY EMEIA, shares examples of how organizations are evolving their functions. In a project with the internationally renowned teaching hospital and research centre Alder Hey Children's Hospital, based in England, she worked on a project with a team of consultants, nurses, psychotherapists and administrative staff. An AI assistant was created for paediatric patients preparing for surgery and provides the opportunity for children to ask questions about their upcoming surgery. The benefits of AI free up resources in the form of stretched staff and provide comfort for children and their families before they face surgery as well as through their stay post-surgery. In her assessment of the project, Selma witnessed individuals who had specific functions around the processes involved being well represented in the inception and development of the project, which had a positive impact on the overall project. By taking a human-centred approach to developing the AI, Turki emphasizes the need for an integrated approach: 'Resources need to be involved and take an active part in the transformation journey. This means that not only the process needs to be clearly defined as part of the strategy, [but] resources, end-users and underlying technology shall be considered as a whole set of elements to help best achieve the expected benefits and end results.'

Most of the conversation about AI focuses on algorithms and accuracy of output being aligned. With increased interaction with consumers, the experience of interaction increasingly becomes as important as the outcome. Previously, AI has been the domain of programmers and coders but as the range of service extended towards developing newer AI, we are now seeing a need for more complexity and variety factored into the programming. Later, we will discuss the impact of diversity, bias and AI in user experiences (Chapter 6), but at this point the questions for you to consider are: How much do you know about AI interactions in your organization? How comfortable are you asking questions about AI and what it means for different functions? What skills do you need to strengthen to engage in AI in a meaningful way? If AI provides the central thrust of disruption to organizations, anyone in any leadership position has a duty to understand what this change means for their teams.

Deborah Richards, former UKI Diversity & Inclusion Lead for IBM, explains the critical skills needed: 'People are going to have to be much more analytical and they're going to be problem solvers. It's going to make work more interesting. I think for those who are working with the data, working with the information, it makes their roles much more strategic because they're going to use technology to provide them with data, with insights and with information. This creates a tension where individuals may have to act in the interest of the client or the business. Previously, they weren't able to analyze vast quantities of unstructured data, but now, they will need to have the skills to interpret the information, to spot trends and to understand what may have been hidden before.'

Without a comprehensive and robust discussion of AI as it develops, the risk is that certain elements of the technology will develop almost in isolation to the practical implementation of the programming. As we have witnessed during the pandemic, decisions around roles and functions, often with cost implications, may emerge quickly without due consideration for wider implications. During a crisis, everyone from the shop floor, new graduates, emerging leaders and chief executives is expected to make critical decisions, knowing that how they manage and implement those decisions will have a lasting impact on an organization. The COVID-19 pandemic dramatically tested the skills of all. Leaders have had to accelerate their speed of thinking on technology adoption and the associated skills development required. They have had to pivot business activity and handle supply chains, rapidly learning how to lead remote teams who adapt to flexible work patterns as well as handling sensitivities of furloughs, redundancies, prioritizing business needs and the healthcare of the workforce. Through all this, they have had to manage their own reputation among all organizational stakeholders, who have been closely observing how they have led and what values they have displayed. Leaders also need to consider what is ahead and major disruptors.

The workplace is adapting at a faster rate due to compressed trends and pronounced differences. Most tech adoption changes are physical, but digital transformations will gather momentum and will be accelerated as companies aim to limit human disruption. Trust motives and privacy will become even more critical and especially focused by how we look at AI from productivity software to digital healthcare. We see that the future could change as new technologies come out of the lab and into businesses, such as 5G, IoT (IoT is the commonly used term for Internet of Things, which encompasses all the technologies that put chips into objects – creating your smart toasters and fridges), Virtual and augmented reality. Andreas Brunner, Chief Executive Officer of Allianz Saudi Fransi, says: 'As a CEO, I know the world is moving fast and COVID-19 had huge impacts on globalization, digitalization and the way we work together across different cultures. All this is based on data provided by humans coming from different cultures with different values and interests. Future leaders must be aware of how to deal with this "input-output relationship" as well as know[ing] how to enrich the outcome. Leaders must use human intelligence of consciousness, creativity and emotionality in order to make sure that the results are beneficial for the social life and individual company targets across countries.'

If you don't have an understanding of what AI means to your function, you are unlikely to be invited to the conversation, which means your role will be transformed without your input. It's the same as your boss working on reclassifying your role without asking you what is important about it and the impact of your work. If you aren't in the driving seat then you're certainly the passenger in your career progression and the driver may not take you to where you expect to end up. There's a lot for emerging leaders to contend with and as many are still at the beginning of this journey, they will turn to subject matter experts in their teams and externally. This is where digital natives have an advantage, as explained by Leanne Wood, Chief Human Resources Officer at Vodafone:

'Millennials and Gen Zs have grown up with technology – it's second nature – and expect to use the same digital tools and have the same control, personalization and flexibility in their work lives. For us at Vodafone, like many other organizations, we were already moving to a more flexible working model and Covid has accelerated this process. In our post-Covid world, I think we're going to see technology playing an increasingly important and positive role in the way we work. With more of us likely to be spending a larger proportion of our time working remotely, technology can be a great enabler of connection and collaboration between colleagues – IoT, 5G and augmented reality will all start to play a bigger role in how we communicate at work.

What are the ethical elements of AI that will impact leadership decisions?

Isaac Asimov (1920–92), the visionary and prolific author of 500 books, including well-known science fiction work that still influences us today, first introduced us to the notion of 'roboethics'. He invented the three laws to govern the behaviour of robots and protect humans:[14]

1) A robot may not injure a human being, or through inaction, allow a human being to come to harm;

---

[14]https://www.scientificamerican.com/article/asimovs-laws-wont-stop-robots-from-harming-humans-so-weve-developed-a-better-solution/

2) A robot must obey the orders given it by human beings except where such orders would conflict with the First Law;

3) A robot must protect its own existence as long as such protection does not conflict with the First or Second Laws.

The laws remain relevant today. However, they are open to a great deal of interpretation when we dig deeper to ask questions around what constitutes harm to an individual and under what circumstances. In fact, Asimov's own stories showed the challenges of robots obeying these rules and when we consider the advancement of AGI and ASI, the chances of following rules seem naive and somewhat redundant.

The complexity around this area is reflected in the evolution of Google's manifesto. During the 2004 IPO, its founders included the statement 'Don't be evil' in the prospectus; this later became known as the 'Don't be evil manifesto'. The document qualified this sentence by stating: 'Don't be evil. We believe strongly that in the long term, we will be better served – as shareholders and in all other ways – by a company that does good things for the world even if we forgo some short-term gains.' In 2018, while the motto was removed from the precast it still remains in the final line of the code of conduct as a reminder of ethical practice: 'And remember... don't be evil, and if you see something that you think isn't right – speak up!'[15] It's worth pointing out that the current mission of Google is: 'Our mission is to organize the

---

[15]Montti, Roger 'Google's "Don't Be Evil" No Longer Prefaces Code of Conduct'. *Search Engine Journal*, retrieved 20 May 2018.

world's information and make it universally accessible and useful.' However, we need to recognize that although there are almost certainly universal laws that we all adhere to, the laws become more complicated when applying norms across the worlds of business, politics, and even education and health. In each sector, we find greater nuances in understanding that 'evil' or 'harm' may be subjective and transient.

The debates around AI and ethics are far-reaching, from the storage and use of data to how results influence our decisions and behaviour. Many people felt at the time, for example, that the work of Cambridge Analytica's role of data analytics and data gathering during the Brexit referendum in the UK in 2016 was unethical and immoral – a fight for what they felt wasn't giving us the truth. Leaving aside the political landscape here, a question we could pose is how did they work out how to exploit our innate human biases and could we instead use AI to illuminate these biases to create fairer systems? In January 2021, social media platforms Facebook and Twitter took the unprecedented step of banning former US President Donald Trump from using their sites following his incitement to storm the Capitol to reject the results of the 2020 US elections. This action in itself poses the question of whether social media sites are merely platforms. Lionel Barber, former Editor of the *Financial Times* tweeted in January 2021: 'Now we can agree that platforms are publishers and that there are some limits to free speech, we need a serious debate about social media's influence in a modern democracy.'[16] The debates around the ethics of social media

---

[16]https://twitter.com/lionelbarber?lang=en

are no longer being held within companies; increasingly, civil society organizations lead the debate – for example, the Center for Humane Technology founded by Tristan Harris, former Design Ethicist at Google, and Aza Raskin, mathematician and dark matter physicist and co-founder of Earth Species Project, is responsible for influencing the next level of this debate.[17]

Across the world, The Alan Turing Institute in the UK and the OECD have started to develop principles for considering AI ethics and the development of regulations and guidelines for a trustworthy use of AI. The drivers for making AI systems more transparent, robust and trustworthy are from consumers, who often say that they feel trust in AI is low – citing a range of concerns, which include worries over the robustness of the AI tools, privacy in terms of people's data and not least biases and discrimination within AI.[18]

As this chapter shows, AI is a tool. But people design, develop and, for the moment, drive the tool. We also know AI is no longer an abstract construct, but something that brings value to every element of our lives. Arijit Mitra, now Head of Innovation at the Institute for Ethical AI as well as Managing Director of his own AI startup, Apurba Ltd, explains the challenges and responsibilities for leaders in handling this transition: 'As an engineer you are looking at the data and you are trying to process the data to a result in order to make it useful to colleagues. To transition data into something useful, engineers need to mould it into a product

---

[17]https://www.humanetech.com/who-we-are#story
[18]https://ec.europa.eu/futurium/en/ai-alliance-consultation/guidelines/1)

or service that can be used. The focus is on the functionality of the data but this can't be developed in isolation, we also need to consider the impact of bias in developing models. These biases become embedded in the emerging models. As a leader you need to understand the impact of these biases and ask some difficult questions around cognitive diversity and data. To start with, "Is my team diverse enough to understand the data to address our customer needs?". The development of AI and the embedded nature of information and data means that it won't stay in the hands of data and AI scientists and engineers. At this formation stage, it is crucial to hardwire ethics and values into thinking and programming. In essence, the values leaders hold will determine the ethics and empathy in AI.

The application of AI is correlated in the direction the CEO wants to go in and its effectiveness will be directly linked to the culture of the organization. For example, if you as a leader may have a goal to produce the best AI as fast as you can and with the best quality, you may want to sacrifice some steps because you fear missing out on market share. This influences how we make decisions and leadership decision making is a critical part of the job as a leader and a huge area of research. It's one reason in business we have a great interest in the fields of neuroscience as we discussed and especially when combined with behavioural science. As we can see in so many business magazines and research journals, we have become fascinated with these areas around psychology because it helps us understand the rationale behind human decisions. While we know artificial intelligence is broadly based on logical, predictive and segmented analysis, it does not have emotional content or context – computers do not understand context (or irony for that matter). Of course there are some incredibly smart AI systems – and there are predictions that AI will be able to write a novel, AI will be able to write a pop song and we will like it because it learned to copy emotion and use syntax well and even sound as though it has emotion and pathos. But AI hasn't had its heart broken to write a killer pop hit like Taylor Swift or experienced loss to pen poetry like Dylan Thomas. AI can't experience the emotion it is projecting. Does it matter? Do we need to feel the author experienced the emotion we share when we listen to their work?

At the start of this chapter we discussed how change is a constant and leadership will also change. As an emerging leader, be mindful of the changes around you and what leadership style you need for the times. One size does not fit all. During a crisis, many leaders, political and business, responded with both empathy and strength. You may want to consider that in relation to your personal growth as we can see purpose and mission-led leadership being highly valued. Critically, in a world that is going to see more AI adoption, coupled with newer working patterns arising from the pandemic, you will need to develop skills in managing uncertainty and building your resilience. There is no doubt the field of AI and ethics is still in its infancy but the pace at which technology is emerging reinforces the urgency for development to occur aligned with the input of multiple stakeholders presenting various valid perspectives. Being cognizant about AI as leaders is not just about the immediate impact of introducing technologies and improving efficiencies, it is about creating value-based frameworks and barriers that protect the essence of the workplace. This requires the creation of a new framework for leadership that is robust in its thinking but flexible enough to adapt to unforeseen innovation.

CHAPTER FOUR

What does the next normal mean for your leadership?

By now, we are pretty comfortable with recognizing that change and disruption to our working lives is inevitable. Irrespective of where your current organization is in this life cycle, you are already riding the storm or you are on the precipice. What matters is how you are handling the change, either as the driver or a passenger. Every organization is facing a threat to the notion of business as usual; we have seen sectors completely brought to a standstill as a result of national lockdowns – tourism, retail, entertainment, any business that relies on bringing in customers to a physical site has experienced disruption to their mode of operating. B2B businesses such as professional services and education have adapted with varying degrees of success to delivering through virtual platforms. Manufacturing and production plants are vulnerable not only because of the markets they serve but also depending on their level of reliance on human workers who have to remain at home during lockdowns. Pivot is another word strongly associated with 2020 as organizations had to adjust to the impact of the global pandemic at lightning speed.

The impact of the global pandemic has unearthed huge inequalities. We've all been in the storm but our experiences vary enormously, whether our vessel is a tiny rowing boat or a sleek yacht and everything else in between. The sense of safety and comfort will be hugely different for everyone and leaders need to be cognizant of this. We mentioned earlier that the health and wellbeing of teams has sky-rocketed in importance for leaders and a big part of this is recognizing that colleagues' experiences of the pandemic will be very different. If we layer on the impact of AI, the impact of experiences becomes even more differentiated. 2020 was a year when organizations experienced exogenous shocks, described by researchers in institutional theory as an unpredicted or unexpected event impacting an organization or even country; the impact of the shock creates waves opening up opportunities for change.

We know exogenous shocks catalyze changes to institutional barriers. An exogenous shock has the same effect as a heart attack on a person and the pandemic has certainly generated this degree of disruption to organizations. Dealing with this level of unprecedented change means finding different, new ways to address the range of problems unleashed on every single organization. New ways in leading, making decisions, creating new processes, implementing and evaluating, refining. The models of change management pretty much flew out of the window as leaders had days in which to react to the scale of changes, with lockdown restricting the movement of people for work, education and entertainment. Organizations that have the experience of handling change are likely to have developed both the resilience and agility to respond to shocks. For some others, usually called 'laggard organizations', they will implement small-scale changes on an ongoing basis (Kondra and Hinings, 1998)[19] and among the others, paradigm stasis sets in, where leaders are unable to perceive the need for change – even in the face of impending threats (Drucker, 1985).[20] Laggards make change, but in his research, Kondra explains that in general change is resisted and in fact leads to defensive strategies against innovators in order to quell the rise of innovative behaviour (Kondra and Hinings, 1998).[21]

For many organizations their current situation is a result of push and pull factors. Their reactions to events in the macro environment pushed them into specific situations – for example, national lockdowns shut down industries. New opportunities emerge from crises where organizations are able to capitalize on emerging technology to test and thrive in new markets. The reality for most organizations is that they are experience a combination of push and pull factors. What matters is how leadership sees the position and identifies opportunities to mobilize talent and resources. Leaders are charged with taking decisive action, crafting a vision for their team and mobilizing resources to shift the narrative into reality. As we discussed in Chapter 1 (*see also* pp. 80–81), distributed leadership occurs across

---

[19]Kondra, A. Z. & Hinings, C. R. (1998) 'Organization diversity and change in Institutional Theory.' *Organisational Studies*; https://doi.org/10.1177/017084069801900502
[20]Drucker, P. F (1985) 'Innovation and Entrepreneurship' *New York Harper and Row*
[21]Op cit.

the organization and is not solely reserved for the higher echelons in the organization. The notion of distributed leadership first emerged in 1999 through James Spillane, Professor in Learning and Organizational Change at Northwestern University.[22]

Distributed leadership describes organizations where individuals across various levels hold leadership responsibility. Creating a distributed model of leadership provides an organizational culture with greater agility and flexibility to respond rapidly to changes. A distributed leadership culture requires specific elements of leadership attributes that are directly opposite to the heroic strongman leadership. Distributed leadership provides the necessary flexibility to draw on different strengths and cognitive diversity from individuals across the organization; this also reminds us that the best talent does not sit at the top of every structure. In Chapter 6, we will dive a bit deeper into creating cultures where cognitive diversity has a chance to thrive and improve business performance.

In organizations with distributed leadership culture the role of the leader shifts from being the autonomous heroic leader who has all the answers to an enabler. In this role, leaders work to create a culture of collaboration and allow teams to build strength and experience in identifying viable solutions. A key element of their role is to remove silos and mental barriers as a way of encouraging teams to collaborate. Laurie Paxton, Chief People Officer for

---

[22]Spillane, J. P. (2012) 'Distributed Leadership' Jossey-Bass, https://www.wiley.com/en-us/Distributed+Leadership-p-9781118429334

Satalia (a distributed tech company), describes her role to achieve this: 'My role is to co-create an organizational environment where our community can thrive. Our purpose is to solve hard problems so everyone is free to live beyond themselves. From a people perspective that means creating an organization that is human-centred, where people have freedom of choice, where they are not constricted by barriers and where people are encouraged to be considerate, curious, creative and courageous. Our community of talented individuals are connected through a passion for creating innovative solutions which will enable our clients to meet the demands for the future of work. My concern is the future of work is being led by the race to digitally transform without designing the transformation with people at its heart. The consequences could be significant. We must collaborate with our employees to design the future of work and ensure we are involving frontline staff whose roles may be automated so they can not only upskill, but also help build effective solutions with their unique insight of the problems customers experience.'

Unpacking this further requires leadership that is comfortable with change, disruption and innovation. The types of organization that represent this kind of behaviour are entrepreneurial companies; startups that are still in their infancy in terms of creating cultures, processes and ways of working. Entrepreneurial leadership is still a very new term, but one that encompasses the key elements of behaviour and attitudes individuals need to navigate their career paths in the next normal. It might seem like an oxymoron to couple the words entrepreneur and leader, but as we have seen the range of disparity in what constitutes leadership behaviour does not always lead to an individual being proactive or decisive in decision making. The characteristics of an entrepreneurial leader speak to an individual who draws on the qualities of being entrepreneurial or enterprising; having an enterprising mindset means being able to see trends and spotting new opportunities that will lead to new ventures and initiatives. If the measure of success is financial then this means spotting commercial opportunities, but it can also mean identifying ways to achieve wider goals, such as those aligned with the United Nations Sustainable Development Goals (SDGs).

Spotting an opportunity is only half the story of success, creating the conditions to act means mobilizing resources; assembling the right talent to understand and implement the plan, ensuring there are additional resources such as finances, technology and time. In addition to these tangible resources, when embarking on a new project, leaders need to mitigate risk, recognize the likelihood of failure (total or partial) and address this in the mindset of the team. We will discuss failure and attitudes towards risk later in Chapter 8 in terms of individuals navigating careers, but at this point the role of a leader is critical in creating an appetite for risk. Embracing change and welcoming innovation cannot and actually will not happen if the leader has not engendered a culture of trust and willingness to let colleagues think about doing things differently. The reality is this behaviour can't spring up overnight, it's not like a tap where you can turn on or turn off creativity; for entrepreneurial leadership to flourish the leader and their team is vested in creating a culture of trust, drip by drip.

Richard Dickson, President and COO of Mattel, Inc., has nurtured creativity across the organization to encourage colleagues to consider creative approaches to new products leading to groundbreaking approaches to toys, challenging gender stereotypes and revitalizing the Barbie range: 'Look, I'm a big believer that creativity is the single most important leadership competency, the future. You know, the ability for us to imagine and or create paths forward. The ability to execute against creativity technology provides data tools, but without the creative skill set to do something with that it is just information alone. Creativity, I believe, is going to be more pronounced across, frankly, every part of leadership. The competency that you need to have to imagine, and use the data and use the information to solve problems, create solutions for consumers whatever it may be, but creativity and the application of that creativity is going to be the real asset of the future. But creativity doesn't emerge until you're brave enough to act on the idea.'

Developing a creative approach and building muscle memory requires creating the practice of creativity. In the second section of the book we will provide specific ways in which you can develop and strengthen your creative skills. Creative thinking often means stepping out of your comfort zone – challenging the status quo and considering how things can be done differently. In order to change behaviour and literally rewire your brain, you need to be clear about the benefits and why it is worth the investment of time and effort.

One of the most challenging aspects associated with being an entrepreneurial leader is encouraging your team to buy into your vision without having total clarity on what the end result looks like. When you factor in the enormity of change in the workplace associated with AI, you start to see how things can become more difficult to navigate. This is where it helps to see a shift in leadership goals to encompass not only what are we going to achieve, but equally importantly, how we will achieve our goals.

When was the last time you consciously thought about your values in the context of work? When have you experienced a situation that crossed a line for you? Did you comply or did you take a stand? Having values may seem like lofty ideals, particularly when the economy is not in a great shape and career prospects are dicey, but as we discussed in Chapter 3 (*see also* pp. 47–67), the pace of change in AI means technology won't wait until you are ready to discuss the ethical implications. Furthermore, if you are asking people to invest their careers and align their brands with your vision and, possibly, untested thinking, they need to feel comfortable that they can trust you. In other words, you will deliver what you say you will and they won't be exposed for having placed their trust in you. If there is one thing we have learnt from the world of social media, it is far easier to make and break professional reputations; we have far greater transparency than ever before, allowing individuals to call out deceptive or disrespectful behaviour.

Today more than ever, more people aspire to lead and more people have the opportunity to step into leadership but the stakes for successful leadership are higher than ever as well. This is partly why the net for leadership is cast even more widely as leadership capabilities to successfully handle these so-called 'wicked problems' require a different skill set than we have previously witnessed. Planning for leadership can seem daunting, particularly in the face of extreme change, but there are things you can do to build your entrepreneurial capabilities. A big element is being able to step back and recognize the opportunities emerging. Once you develop this practice of spotting emergent trends, you strengthen this approach to creative thinking and making connections that keep you in the driving seat. Sir John Chisholm, Executive Chair at Genomics England, has built his career from spotting trends and creating new opportunities: 'When it comes to thinking about how to make a difference in the world, then a big piece is knowing how you use your knowledge and insights as your guiding principle to make decisions rather than jumping to opportunities. I don't think you need to train yourself too hard, you just need to be thoughtful about what you read, what it means. Be prepared to learn from others and to admit the idea you had last week wasn't exactly right and be prepared to experience discomfort in the short term because you have to take on challenges which you probably didn't expect.'

Later in this book, we will discuss the specific elements you can pay attention to in developing your skills as an entrepreneurial leader. Before we move on to this, let's take a moment to consider the key elements of what leadership is. In Chapter 1 we discussed leadership as an activity (*see also* pp. 9–25) – in fact, it's a series of activities but quite often when we talk about leadership, we conflate the behaviour with the attitudes and traits. It's fair to say most people will agree leadership is about setting a goal and moving a team of people towards that goal. Even within this relatively simplistic description there are hundreds, if not thousands, of decisions about how these steps are achieved. Let's break leadership activity down into four main areas, illustrated in the diagram below:

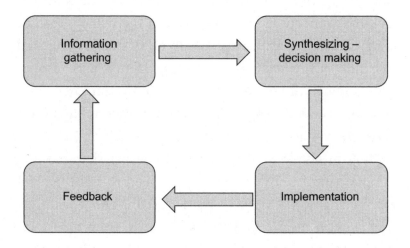

Fundamentally, this model represents leadership activity and it's quite straightforward but the really interesting piece happens in detail not only in the boxes but also in the arrows. Let's briefly examine each of the boxes.

Information gathering: On a regular basis, where do you access information? Here are some common examples:

Industry reports and journals
Market dynamics
Industry conferences/workshops
Thought leaders/subject matter experts
Team members/colleagues
Wider network from other sectors
General data reports

As you run through this list you can probably add more sources of information but there are some really interesting questions for you to consider as well:

- When you are exposed to new information that contradicts your thinking, how much do you absorb?
- How often do you consciously seek out new information that challenges your assumptions?
- How do you make time on a regular basis to acquire new information?
- How do you use new information in your thinking?
- What do you do with information that doesn't resonate with your views?

Decision making: a lot of the models on leadership focus on the behaviour and nature of how leaders make decisions. How you absorb information will impact how you make decisions and is likely to be linked to your preferred style of learning (more of that in Chapter 9). Here are a few more questions to consider:

- How comfortable are you in generating big sweeping ideas?
- How do you handle ongoing incremental change?
- How do you usually reach a decision? Do you spend time reflecting on your own or does your light-bulb moment come when you are discussing ideas with someone else?
- What does collaboration mean to you?
- How comfortable are you with sharing ideas and suggestions and taking on board different perspectives?

Of course, with decision making comes accountability – decisions are not made in isolation and one of the most challenging aspects when stepping into leadership is the responsibility. It can be easy to get caught up in importance and dare we say, status of leadership, being heard and considered, but without accountability, leadership doesn't exist. Even with the emergence of leadership through collaboration, responsibility still lies with someone. Working together in a partnership or with a group is fraught with dynamics and different levels of commitment but at the end of the day, there is a need for clarity and conversations to ensure the work is done.

When it comes to implementation and execution, there is a view this is less about leadership and more to do with managers. But in organizations with distributed leadership, implementation occurs at all levels rather than having senior leadership issue dictates for managers to implement. You may or may not be directly responsible for the implementation but you will still need to ensure the vision and plan is clearly communicated, understood and absorbed, and the necessary resources are in place for this goal to be achieved. Nothing is more demoralizing than building a fantastic castle and then not equipping your team to go ahead and realize that vision. Different leadership styles again focus on the degree of control leaders have on implementation, their ability to delegate or at the other extreme, micromanaging daily activities.

A few more questions to consider:

- How comfortable are you trying different approaches to working with a team in the implementation phase?
- How often do you reflect on different leadership approaches and incorporate these elements into your style?
- How open are you with your team in experimenting with new approaches of working?

Personal experience of leaders and the degree of comfort in your teams is a huge element in the style of leadership you develop. What also makes a significant difference is the impact of role models and how senior leaders have helped to shape your approach.

Closing the loop – feedback is essential to all of us, not only in terms of whether we successfully achieve expected goals but also focusing on the experience for yourself and your colleagues. Reflecting on feedback is essential in building self-efficacy, which is an incredibly important element for stretching in leadership roles and again an area for which we will provide a deeper dive in Chapter 9.

A few more questions for you to consider in relation to the feedback loop:

- How often do you proactively seek feedback beyond formalized performance reviews?
- How do you seek feedback from colleagues whom you don't normally choose to engage with?
- How often do you come back to your feedback and reflect on what this means for your leadership approach?
- How comfortable are your colleagues in providing honest feedback to you?

Netflix is a company that has made constructive feedback core to its culture by fostering a culture of candour in the way feedback is given and received. In their book, *No Rules Rules: Netflix and the Culture of Reinvention*, Netflix CEO Reed Hastings and INSEAD Professor Erin Meyer shared the four As – the principles to create a strong feedback culture:

Aim to assist – clearly explain how a specific behaviour change will help the team/organization;

Actionable – what the recipient can do differently;

Appreciate – value the feedback that has been received;

Accept or discard – active listening and consider the feedback. The receiver has control over their decision to act or not.

There is a fifth A – **Adaptation** – cultivating a culture of radical openness, which requires deep trust within teams and across the organization.

We will probe more deeply into these areas in the subsequent chapters where we discuss leadership tools. Before we do this, it's important to consider how the leadership process will be impacted by emerging trends in organizations as a result of AI. There are three specific areas to focus on:

1) Increased complexity: the rise of 'wicked problems' analysis (inequalities/wider stakeholder groups);
2) New skill sets involved in strategic thinking – data handling and mitigating for bias in AI;
3) The impact of different working models on organization culture: hybrid and remote working.

Increased complexity

A strong change agenda needs to consider the perspectives of wider stakeholders and environmental factors to conduct a sense-making analysis. At some point you will need to get specific and understand the implications of AI in your sector and your profession but this has to be in tandem with understanding what is happening in the wider environment. Going in deep and narrow inevitably leads to silo thinking, which can be difficult to emerge from and will reduce the likelihood of effective innovation through collaboration (Chapter 6). When we talk about sense-making, this is an approach for leaders to understand the environment in which they live and work. It means building the skill of multiple perspectives; a bit like driving – keeping an eye on what is happening immediately in front of you (possibly also behind you), but also looking further to see what is ahead. As a leader, developing multiple perspectives is a skill and can be challenging when you are used to focusing on details. Leading in an increasingly complicated environment requires making sense of the world, but also being comfortable with not having all the answers. Being OK with uncertainty is perhaps one of the most challenging aspects for leaders, particularly if we are used to working in organizations where the leader is expected to provide stability and clear responses.

Being comfortable with uncertainty is not the same as being totally clueless about the situation and this is where sense-making is essential. Sense-making, developed by American organizational therapist Karl E. Weick, is a framework to help leaders create a staged approach to uncertainty in order to make decisions with some certainty. The key to sense-making is to create a plausible understanding of a world in flux and begins with data collection.

Data handling and mitigating for bias

Your ability to handle data is more important than ever before. It's now the fuel for effective strategic planning, so much so that we have dedicated a chapter in this book to understanding data as a critical skill for leadership. Each organization, department and team has unique data and access to far more data than ever before. Data handling is not a single process; how it is gathered, how it is cleaned and whether it is subject to the biases deal with the first part, but then what you do with the data is also important. Data is more than presenting facts and figures, it's about building a narrative that creates connection and security, particularly when you are navigating through an uncertain path.

Bias is another area that has sky-rocketed over the last few years; most of us are familiar with bias under the diversity agenda but the impact of bias in our thinking is considerable when discussing data and how we use it to make business decisions. Understanding bias and its implications cannot be overestimated for leaders and so we spend time in Chapter 6 explaining the importance of creating a pluralistic culture in teams where cognitive diversity thrives and helps to create better-quality data to improve decision making.

The impact of different working models on organization culture

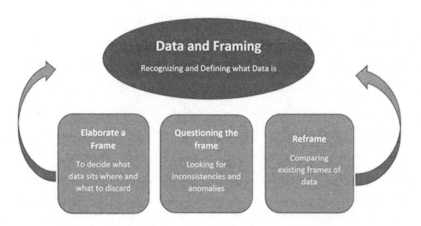

An adapted version of data/framing model (after Klein, 2006).

The impact of different working models on organization culture: gig, hybrid and remote working

Working from home over a long period is classed as remote working, whereas hybrid working blends being in the workplace and remote working. With more people having experienced remote or hybrid working throughout 2020, this pattern is likely to rise in the coming years but the shift will not occur uniformly across all sectors or globally. The surge in research around remote working often produced conflicting results demonstrating the confusion in how everyone was adapting to a situation without a blueprint. Let's look at some of the key statistics from the World Economic Forum (WEF). Ninety-eight per cent of people surveyed said that they would like to have the option to work remotely for the remainder of their careers. Fifty-seven per cent of senior leaders prefer traditional working approaches, but this figure shows that just under half adapted to flexible working very quickly. Over half of the global workforce (63 per cent) felt they were more productive working from home than when they worked in an office.[23]

Inevitably, wider research on remote working demonstrates different reactions to changes in working patterns. As shared in Chapter 1 (*see also* pp. 9–25), research by Boston Consulting Group found during the first phase of lockdown in spring 2020 there was an increased strain on women shouldering the domestic burden. The mental health implications showed two-thirds of women and just over half of the men

---

[23]https://www.weforum.org/reports/the-future-of-jobs-report-2020

(52 per cent) expressed concerns about their mental health. The contrasting statistics in this section highlight the level of inequality experienced by workers as a result of remote working during COVID-19. Beyond these stats there are multiple discussion points – the benefits of autonomy, not being micromanaged, creating different work-family dynamics, more flexibility to take up hobbies/exercise.

Commuting represents a big piece of this discussion: a team of researchers from Chicago examined the impact of COVID-19 on work-related travel. Eighty-two per cent of new teleworkers felt no commuting had a positive influence on working. Of course, where a virus is not under control, travelling on public transport or taking taxi rides raises fears about transmission, aggravating further reluctance to revive the daily commute. Attitudes towards commuting are also linked to 'home workability', as described by Ali Shamshiripour, a researcher at the University of Illinois, and his research team to explain distractions and a lack of comfortable working environment at home.[24] Home workability refers to the home environment providing comfortable and energetic working spaces with the opportunities for restful breaks and minimal disruptions. If your experiences of working from home are similar to the descriptions aligned with 'home workability', it is likely that you are more open to remote working over the longer term.

---

[24]Shamshiripour, A., Rahimi, E., Shabanour, R. & Mohammadian, A.K. (2020) 'How is Covid-19 reshaping activity-travel behaviour? Evidence from a comprehensive survey in Chicago.' *Transportation Research Interdisciplinary Perspectives*, 7, https://doi.org/10.1016/j.trip.2020.100216

Gig working (working on short-term or 'zero-hours' contracts, where work is not guaranteed) focuses different attention on our experiences of working and even if you aren't a gig worker, the chances are someone in your team falls into this category. Gig working demands even more attention being placed on empathetic skills among teams to ensure members feel involved and contribute to the bigger picture (remember the NASA janitor from Chapter 2?). Individuals who become gig workers demonstrate high levels of intrinsic motivation, describing high levels of self-motivation and self-determination. This work is presented in self-determination theory (SDT), an area that has become more active in the social psychology field of research since the 2000s. Work by Emeritus Professor Richard Ryan and Professor Edward Deci, both from the University of Rochester in New York, has shaped SDT since the 1970s. Applying SDT to gig work reinforces the importance of workers needing connection and loyalty to their organization. In a recent survey of 250 gig workers, the results showed that satisfaction of work is affected by self-determination and the characteristics of their job. In their model, the experiences of working build and reinforce motivation, engagement and volition, leading to enhanced performance and persistence.

Will distributed workforces be the big thing in the future of work?

Probably not, but they will take a bigger piece of the workplace pie. The shift to remote work for businesses that could move to this showed that much of their delivery could continue and in some ways it worked better, perhaps furthering the idea that distributed workplaces will surge ahead. It's important to note that it's not just having workers in separate locations that makes a distributed workforce, the infrastructure of fluid autonomous work culture is the key driver. For this type of operation to work, not only does there need to be a high level of trust-building, but also a high level of team nurturing done through formal training and informal mentoring and championing. A report by EY suggests that the attraction of distributed workforces isn't just that workers can work at home or in co-working spaces, but they are seen as valuable knowledge workers.[25] One key reason workers enjoy being part of a distributed company is because they are seen and shown to be critical to the business. Workers are also encouraged to have a range of different career paths, possibly even to work in other organizations too.

It sounds obvious and the kind of thing we expect in non-distributed teams, but all too often workers in many regular organizations feel they are less significant or stand-out. Traditional companies are considering models to give more flexibility, e.g. support side hustling and offer a 4DayWeek. Will distributed work become the norm? It's unlikely in the short term for two reasons: 1) the experiences of various lockdowns showed that while work could be done through a distributed work model, the desire to belong to something

---

[25]https://www.ey.com/en_ca/workforce/leveraging-a-distributed-workforce-model-to-accelerate-your-busi

(often to a physical place with people) was missing – and this reduced job satisfaction; 2) the leadership skills needed to motivate a distributed workforce are specific and need time to develop a different way of connecting and building relationships.

The importance of these non-traditional models of work show there's a core motivational need for people to still have a connection to work and workplaces, even if they are 'free and fluid', and can contribute in a meaningful manner, as identified by Daniel Hulme, CEO of Satalia: 'My job is to define the vision and purpose of Satalia. I need to ensure we have an organization that is distributed in structure and also sustainable and scalable, and to ensure that we are aligned and delivering towards that vision. Satalia's purpose is to solve hard problems; in particular, creating solutions that remove frictions from the process of innovation.'

People still want an anchor. As self-determination theory (SDT) shows, even in autonomy, people need a sense of relatedness and they still need to be motivated and engaged. SDT motivational theory says that three psychological needs are necessary for us to have higher motivation: 1) competence, 2) autonomy and 3) relatedness. Autonomy and competence are obviously part of gig/distributed work – but relatedness? Yes, we still need to belong. The research study on gig workers showed SDT and in particular the sense of 'belonging' that comes from relatedness was a critical aspect that influenced both joy and performance Even in gig, remote and distributed work, we still want to feel part of an organization, feel aligned to its values and purpose, as well as enjoying the benefits of working with others, and leaders need to be mindful of this need.

New work ahead?

The experience of the global pandemic has meant some organizations cannot work remotely – those in health, transport and food manufacturing, to mention a few. The pandemic also drove many other organizations into remote working, usually from home. This move to remote working created a lot of opportunities to examine where work might happen in the future. Naeema's research on lockdown working conducted in the summer of 2020 surveyed human resource (HR) managers and directors. It showed that despite the apparent enjoyment of autonomous remote working, most workers like working with other people in a physical space – indicating that calls for knocking down offices might be misplaced. She surveyed two groups: one was HR leaders in a major finance company and the other mixed the participants with a range of organizations with HR leaders, from small organizations to large multinational companies. The study was qualitative and so questions were posed on how the impact of remote working influenced their workers and asked participants to think about them and answer in their own words. These results were then analyzed for any strong and clear themes emerging from the answers.

Interestingly, the results from both groups were the same: most people enjoyed spending less time on long commutes. They also showed that people like some aspects of remote work as in some ways it was 'humanizing'. Workers said they enjoyed seeing the informality of the CEOs working from home and dressed more casually and also the special appearance of a small child or pet. The research highlighted that employees developed greater empathy for their leader as the situation reinforced a more human approach to working. However, universally, all said that they found collaboration and doing more creative activity difficult, as well as being able to care for colleagues going through hard times. The absence of informal chats over coffee and at the watercooler were the things people missed most, despite having virtual coffee and cake breaks with colleagues. The workplace, it seemed, offers a way of teaming, caring and creating. And feeling part of real social networks is important, not least to experience a sense of belonging and identity – these features were especially highlighted as being needed by younger workers.

We will probably see greater hybrid working emerging (where organizations will construct work to be done in both workplaces and homes, offering more flexibility). This new structure not only covers changes in the workplace, but also home working or flexible working spaces, as well as transport and travel patterns. As an emerging leader, there are three key aspects you need to think about as you consider flexible working for your teams:

1) What effect does remote/hybrid/workplace working have on your sense of self as a worker? What impact did it have on aspects of your non-work persona, which may now feature in your virtual working life?

2) Wherever your work took place during the pandemic (remote/hybrid/workplace), what were your experiences with your leader(s) and also with your teams? What effort did you make to create a connection; how did you encourage colleagues to keep connected – such as keeping screens on during a video call? For your quieter or more introverted colleagues, how did you encourage their contribution to discussions? How did you discuss concerns and pressures if you were still working in a workplace? How did being furloughed affect your self-image? How did you consciously create ways to amplify your human side as a leader or colleague?

Finally, in remote and hybrid working, leadership support is invaluable. Despite staff enjoying the autonomy of working remotely, they still need support. In these situations, the balance between supervising or being too remote creates additional needs for leaders to build empathy for team members. Empathetic leadership is high on the radar, as we discuss in Chapter 9, but developing empathetic skills takes time. It isn't a cookie-cutter approach, applying leadership in a single manner without adapting to the environment. Effective empathy has to be authentic and in your style otherwise you lose the basis of trust and honesty, both of which are essential for these relationships to flourish.

In this chapter we have pulled together different elements of emerging technology, along with the ramifications of the pandemic on changing how we work and, more importantly, the implications for leaders. This wave of change has created the opportunity to reconsider leadership approaches more suited to a distributed organization and culture, along with being more adept at anticipating and handling change. As we have discussed here, entrepreneurial leadership is not about leading startups, but extracts the behaviours and styles that are essential in helping a startup navigate the early stages of uncertainty to grow into robust, innovative business.

In the next section of the book, we will get even more practical around leadership styles and attributes to help you create a toolkit for your leadership. As with any toolkit, dip in and out of the material, make notes to take actions regarding areas where you want to pay more attention to your leadership development. Above all, we are going to challenge you with difficult questions and encourage you not to shy away from those areas that make you feel uncomfortable, but instead to embrace the questions and topics and figure out how you stretch your personal comfort zone.

CHAPTER FIVE

Developing career resilience

When it comes to developing your career, we agree that it can sometimes feel like it's a bit of a minefield. While an organization is there to support you, you must be in the driving seat of your career – you can no longer rely on the notion that your company will take care of you. That almost paternalistic role disappeared at the end of the third industrial revolution with the advent of more decentralized and flatter organizational structures, and with the rise of the entrepreneurial leader. New work in this new world of work requires us all to be more self-reliant, not least with the rise of AI and automation

Becoming a leader is aligned with career progression and this in itself requires the approach we discussed in Chapter 4: constantly scanning for new information, new trends and challenging your assumptions to see different opportunities and prospects (*see also* pp. 69–94). Of course, it is inevitable there are times when handling your work and responsibilities can seem daunting and overwhelming; at some point, everyone has experienced hitting a wall when it just feels like hard work to keep going. But let's return to those important questions – not so much what do you want to do, but what impact do you want to make? How can your work help you to achieve this? Trying out new ways of thinking, developing skills as an entrepreneurial leader means you will make mistakes – in fact, if you're not making mistakes, you're probably not being bold enough. Making mistakes is inevitable, taking responsibility and learning from those mistakes is far more difficult, but as we'll discuss in this chapter there are certain themes in the behaviours and beliefs of people who overcome failure and achieve success. A central theme to this chapter is the importance of resilience for our careers (no candles and breathing exercises listed, but sure, go ahead and bring them in, if you like). In this discussion, we demonstrate why encouraging and maintaining risk is essential to career resilience.

When you hear or read the word 'resilience', what reaction does it elicit for you? It's become a word we see a lot more, to maybe the point of overuse. And while we all have a sense of what it means, have you really thought about what it means for you? How does it make you feel when you are asked to be more resilient? What skills and attitudes do you need to draw upon? What behaviour demonstrates your resilience? Resilience is an important trait for leaders to withstand the pressures they face for themselves and their teams, particularly during times of intense turbulence and uncertainty. Building resilience allows us to bounce back *and* rebuild (sometimes better than before), when we get knocked or events don't go as planned.

It's important to recognize *career resilience* specifically is important, but if we understand what constitutes resilience in general then we have a better chance of navigating new areas, being more comfortable with taking risks and bouncing back when things do go awry, while learning from those experiences to propel us into new, uncharted territory. Before we focus on career resilience, then, let's do a deep dive into resilience and what constitutes this behaviour.

Resilience clusters together a range of behaviours that help us to keep ploughing forwards. There are seven specific attitudes and associated behaviours identified by Alex Davda (2017). Here, we illustrate the attitudes along with questions for you to consider for each one in the table below. We have provided space for you to note down your responses – it's worth spending some time thinking about these questions.

Build personal resilience: key factors

Purpose		
The extent to which you have structure, commitment and meaning present in your life	What would you describe as your legacy?	How often do you reflect on this question and change your response?
Challenge		
How you perceive situations, solve problems and manage change	How do you react to unexpected changes?	How often do you seek out change in your career/personal life?
Emotional control		
The way in which you control your emotions and how you attribute this control	How easy do you find it to maintain control of your emotions under stressful situations?	What do you practise to build control over your emotions?

Balance		
How you choose to view the world and the attention given to aspects in your life	Using a tool such as the Wheel of Life, where you draw a circle, divide it into segments, and label key aspects of your life around each segment, then give each one a score, consider what needs to change, when, and how, to decide what to prioritize in your life.	When you need to change priorities, does the change come from within or external factors?
Self-determination		
Your ability to remain motivated and bounce back after difficulty	How often do you see a project through with enthusiasm?	What factors lead to you giving up on projects?
Self-awareness		
Your belief in your capabilities and the accuracy of these self-estimations	When colleagues or friends describe you, do you relate to their descriptions of you?	How often do you experience imposter syndrome?
Interpersonal confidence		
Your awareness of others; how you communicate, interact and empathize with them	How often do you receive feedback on how you have impacted colleagues in terms of motivation?	When working in teams, how often do you 'scan' the team to gauge emotions and regulate yourself accordingly?

Some of your responses may surprise you and depending on how honest you have been, some may be quite uncomfortable, too. Even for us, as co-authors, every time we review these questions, there are always a few responses where we know we need to pay more attention. The good news is each of these areas can be improved and in doing so, this strengthens the foundations for resilience. We think this approach is helpful as it breaks down the enormity of resilience and provides you with the opportunity to go into more detail when it comes to the specific areas you can pay attention to. If you examine these areas more closely, you will see the common thread of self-managing, which again requires discipline and attention. If you are really keen to see the impact of progress, set yourself a diary reminder to come back to these questions in six months and reflect on what has changed for you – you'll probably be quite surprised at the impact of change when you pay attention to specific areas.

Neeti Shukla of Automation Anywhere shares the importance of resilience in emerging tech when leaders are playing the long game: 'Resiliency is the name of the game. This will be a key attribute for leaders moving forward. We need to upskill leaders and train them to make their organizations resilient. As we build greater flexibility into end-to-end value chains and achieve success in the face of volatility and uncertainty, it will require leadership that is agile and creative. Organizations will require leaders to bring in best practices and tried-and-tested methods as needed, while thinking out of the box to create breakthroughs in times of crisis. Success requires unwavering faith in your vision and terrific leadership. We are just now seeing explosive growth in the RPA [robotic process automation] industry. What people don't realize is that we spent more than a decade building up to this point, and in that time, we dealt with countless sceptics who did not understand or believe in our vision of implementing software bots to automate tasks and enhance human workers. Failure is a part of success and sometimes creating a technology product that the market isn't ready for or the technology can have several false starts. Understand the failure to move forward and recognize that the possibilities are endless, in good times and even in times of crises. I have found that staying positive is key. Don't let setbacks bring you down and don't lose sight of your goals. Remember, you will get where you are going and don't doubt it.'

As you become more confident in spotting opportunities, you also start to become more discerning in which ideas you want to grab. We all know what it's like to work with someone (or we may know what it's like to be that person) who spots opportunities and generates dozens of ideas. The buzz of new ideas is addictive but it can be exhausting (and be mindful, it can also be demoralizing for colleagues). This does not mean we want unemotional leaders who don't display signs of excitement, but we want leaders and colleagues who can self-manage their emotions too. We are going to spend a bit of time discussing how our brains react to change but before we do that, let's consider the contagion of emotions. Human beings as a species are highly receptive to emotions – it's part of our survival behaviour built from our primal brain. Emotions can be picked up through non-verbal signals in milliseconds. Once we've subconsciously acknowledged the emotion, we are very likely to respond and mimic that emotion. It is perhaps no surprise that most of our emotions are negative, as illustrated in the diagram below:

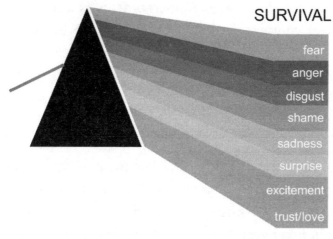

Image adapted from Swart, Chisholm and Brown[26]

Our survival has been reliant on our ability to draw upon emotions that led to the fight-or-flight reactions. We have two dominant emotions for positive experiences (joy and happiness) and one that is neutral – surprise. Think about the last time you attended a surprise party (that was a genuine shock) and the reality that the outcome could have gone either way. More often than not, when this information is shared with leaders in training sessions participants are

[26]Swart, T., Chisholm, K. and Brown, P. (2015) *Neuroscience for Leadership: Harnessing the brain gain advantage*, Hampshire Palgrave Macmillan.

not surprised. More importantly, once this is acknowledged the important recurring question is 'So how do we manage ourselves and our emotions for our teams?' or 'How do we become better equipped at self-management?'

Building self-management is a continuous process and adapting to changing environments is a learned skill requiring constant attention. Throughout this book we have discussed the impact of turbulence and change in the wider environment, along with adaptability and agility in careers, all of which result in a great deal of uncertainty. Developing and strengthening resilience needs to be a priority for emerging leaders as frankly, when you are in leadership roles, it's too late to start thinking about the coping mechanism and leadership traits you wish to nurture. Former US First Lady Michelle Obama shares her view on leadership in her memoir, *Becoming*: 'Presidency doesn't change who you are, it reveals who you are. You are flying at such high altitude you don't have time for change.' While we don't promote the super-hero model of leadership, we do believe in super-hero resilience qualities that are essential for successful leadership and top of the list is *adaptability*.

Managing in uncertainty – how our brains help and hinder

Our brain neurotransmitters release a hormone called dopamine, which you probably have heard about – it's the one that enables us to get gratification from pleasure (nice). And you've probably heard that the roller coaster of pleasure emotions can sometimes be addictive too (not so nice). However, dopamine also has another role: it actually drives us away from negative outcomes and it's these dopamine ups and downs in the brain that can contribute to stress when we are working in uncertainty. So much so, it can often feel more stressful not knowing an outcome than the outcome itself.

But there is even more to our brain chemistry. When we are expecting bad news, for example, the dopamine gets our brain working on various possible scenarios to work out ways we can manage the odds – as the brain imagines good and bad consequences. A result of the uncertainty associated with stress is heightened levels of cortisol. This fight-or-flight hormone can lead to your brain closing down on lateral thinking as it strives to survive and focus on the source of threat. As you can see, there is a very delicate balance to uncertainty – cortisol and stress will shut down our thinking, while dopamine encourages us to promote new thinking and often create our best work. When we understand how our reactions impact the outcomes for our careers then we also recognize why self-management is essential for career success.

Handling uncertainty is not easy by any stretch, so let's get specific about how we can reduce uncertainty by understanding what we can mitigate. Understanding emerging tech and developments in AI is essential (if you skipped Chapter 3, pp. 47–67, which focused on this area, now would be a good time to go back and get familiar with the current trends in emerging tech). As you become more familiar with the different emerging technologies and their impact in our lives, you will have a much greater grasp of the opportunities ahead. Getting more familiar with emerging technology helps mitigate the uncertainty and by becoming part of the conversation, you can shift from managing stress to creative solutions about how to engage with tech in your functions. The more you know and the more you shape thinking, the greater your acumen in understanding emerging tech and this is when you are more likely to move into leadership opportunities. Fear doesn't create the optimal conditions for new learning, and as we discuss in Chapter 9, successful learning experiences are strongly correlated with intrinsic motivation. Developing curiosity when it comes to new learning undoubtedly helps the production of dopamine, which in turn creates a virtuous cycle; when we adopt new knowledge in a curious and open manner, we make connections for new projects and opportunities that will inevitably benefit our careers.

In a world of increasing complexity, leaders need to take clear, unambiguous decisions that have a strong data and evidence base and incorporate diverse thinking. If we consider the impact of decisions of political leaders during the first six months of the pandemic in 2020, we witnessed lower levels of COVID-19 cases and Covid-related deaths in countries with female leaders. Research from the universities of Reading and Liverpool showed that countries with male leaders experienced double the number of fatalities compared to female-led countries: Australia, Finland, Germany and Taiwan. In this analysis of the research, female leaders demonstrated specific behaviours in response to a sudden and rapid rise of uncertainty, using science-driven data to determine what was happening, making decisions quickly and effectively. The 'risk' was acting quickly and decisively on policies without knowing how the situation would unfold. The key takeaway from this research is the competency and speed of leaders making decisions even when all the information is unknown. In the face of increased uncertainty, this leadership trait becomes even more essential for entrepreneurial leaders to engender trust and stability.

Sumati Sharma, who is Partner at Oliver Wyman and Chair of Women in Aviation explains the need to build competence and confidence with resilience: 'We need to become even more comfortable with resilience in rapidly changing environments. Technology along with the global crisis has brought rapid and constant changes and we have seen situations change by the day or even by the hour. We are adapting to many changes so fast on both individual and corporate levels – changes that affect our work, personal and family life, wellbeing and health. These changes are coming from every direction, government, health authorities, workplace and community, and it is a role of leaders to manage through these changes, making sure that their team is supported, flexible and up-to-date with new technologies.'

Cultivating career resilience

Focusing specifically on career resilience gives you even more focus and provides a lens on your leadership development. Career resilience throws up many positive attributes and skills you need to build a successful career and develop the skills to become an effective entrepreneurial leader, particularly in turbulent environments. The range of skills includes: flexibility in attitudes towards roles and opportunities, nurturing a growth mindset, cultivating positivity for yourself and colleagues working with you, consistently clear communication. As you review these areas again, you can see clear connections emerging. With an open mindset, you are more likely to spot and act on new opportunities and with a growth mindset, you will take on new challenges with a positive appetite.

In order to investigate this important area, Naeema conducted a long-term study of career resilience as part of her doctoral studies over a period of three years, tracking people through their studies and into their jobs. The study had around a 50:50 split of males to females and a broad mix of different nationalities and ethnicities. But for research homogeneity purposes (i.e. to make good comparisons and investigate correlations), they all had similar qualifications and work experience. She analyzed the difference in resilience that people displayed and looked at factors influencing that. When she added in control factors (e.g. age, ethnicity and gender), she found they didn't have an impact, but a set of other personal qualities did. From this study, she was able to develop a career resilience tool based on the factors that arose. What she found was supported strongly in the academic literature when it comes to career resilience – who you are 'inside' counts most.

Career self-resilience has also been described as having a very self-governing approach to the extent that the individual demonstrates an attitude of self-employment in whatever work they do and we would argue that 'career self-reliance' is an essential quality in career management as it requires individuals to remain open to opportunities and display flexibility in the management of their careers. A crucial part of career self-reliance is that individuals can maintain learning opportunities and create and maintain networks. If an individual is 'career self-reliant', they will ensure that they maintain their career skill set against what the employment market expects, both for future jobs and current employment. This means developing new skills as appropriate and thus, continuously to be assessing new learning opportunities. Naeema breaks career resilience into five factors:

Career Resilience (Pasha 5 Factor Scale)

| POSITIVE SELF-CONCEPT | ADAPTABILITY & RISK | SELF RELIANCE | AMBITION & NETWORKING | MOTIVATION TO LEARN |

Pasha, 2019[27]

Factor 1: Positive Self-concept measured the ability of participants to measure their own skills. It also measured the ability to maintain knowledge of career field in terms of skills and awareness of needing to upgrade skills and abilities to maintain employability, as well as the ability to handle career problems by extending skills.

---

[27]Pasha, N. 'Responding to career uncertainty: Applying a "dual-empathy" approach to career development using corporate strategy theory.' (2020).

Factor 2: Adaptability and Risk measured the extent of handling job and organizational changes; it also measured the ability to take risks and actions with an uncertain outcome. It measured being able to adapt to changing circumstances, too.

Factor 3: Self-reliance measured the extent of having outlined ways of accomplishing jobs without waiting for outside guidance, such as a senior leader. It also measured the ability to put forward ideas and changes to others even though they might disagree, and the ability to self-evaluate performance against personal standards rather than comparing it with what others do.

Factor 4: Ambition and Networking measured the extent of having career goals that are clear and future-focused. It also measured the ability to look for opportunities to interact with people who might be supportive and influential, as well as the ability to identify the future direction of a career field by making personal contacts, reading up on sector and job influences or attending professional meetings – on a regular basis.

Factor 5: Motivation to Learn measured the ability to identify what actions are needed to learn to develop and improve skills and abilities. It also measured the extent to which an individual will actively seek out the learning opportunity (such as reading, taking courses, learning on the job or attending conferences and workshops to learn new knowledge or skills).

Let's now unpack each part:

1. Positive Self-concept

People who understand themselves well by knowing their abilities and the areas they need to build on will have a higher internal locus of control. This means they feel they have a certain control and agency over their careers. If you can relate to this, it is highly likely that you generate creativity and initiate new ideas.

Having a positive self-concept strengthens your resilience and your self-efficacy (your self-esteem). Building self-understanding helps to build your career resilience. Your self-understanding will continue to change and evolve and to do this well, you need to keep reviewing your progress, working out where you excel. Regular progress means a review every six months and asking yourself what makes you, you. What are the simple ways you can do this? Update your CV or your LinkedIn profile. If nothing changes in six months, ask yourself if you are doing enough for your career development. For some of you, self-promotion is extremely uncomfortable, to the point where you will avoid it at all costs. If you are a classic avoider then ask trusted friends or colleagues who can provide constructive feedback, how would they pitch you to a new contact? What skills can you amplify further? What skills do you need to pay more attention to for your own career development?

You can do this by updating your CV/resume, your LinkedIn profile, or your little notebook of what makes you brilliant. Add in your work skills that are technical and applied as well. Review, update, but please, know what you are good at.

2. Adaptability and Risk

Building comfort with uncertainty creates a stronger base for individuals to become adaptable and take risks. Risk-taking is inextricably linked with innovation – to create new ideas, we need to be willing to think differently and break things better. In Chapter 6, we discuss how leaders can create conditions to cultivate innovation. In the context of uncertainty around work, increased risk-taking is necessary for career resilience.

Adaptability and risk is linked to levels of self-confidence as this will determine how experimental you are in your thinking. Risk and adaptability will be linked to how you set your goals: what is realistic and what is ambitious for you? This is the part where you start thinking about how adaptable you are. Your level of comfort and capabilities when you take risks. Remember the growth mindset we discussed earlier? This is where the muscle skills in confidence grow with stretch roles and opportunities. A prerequisite to successful risk-taking means building a tolerance for failure; in our world of media-hyped celebrity leadership, it seems individuals have walked a gilded path to success. We discuss failure and leadership later in this chapter.

Essentially, here, you will start to attribute success to trying out something, having an ability to think it's OK to recognize failure as learning, and not just be thinking about the outcome. We know being adaptive to new opportunities is a massive part of working in the new world of work and risk-taking (measured risks, of course) enables you to develop a tolerance of uncertainty and ambiguity and makes you more experimental. It will also give you a sense of being the manager of your career, so try taking small risks. If that feels strange, do it anyway and know that it's OK to get things wrong.

3. Self-reliance

Autonomy or independence is also important as it enables individuals to create agency over their career path. Where individuals exercise their choice, they are likely to experience lower stress levels and feel happier.

This is a big one: the study found that people who built a stronger sense of self-reliance (thinking they can achieve things) also build stronger career self-management. Again, it's also how you build your self-efficacy. In feeling you have accountability for your actions, you own your career and you can be in control and will build your resilience and ability to withstand change in your job.

Leadership is also about accountability and knowing that it's down to you to set the outcome expectations you have of yourself. Self-reliant people often take a goal and find themselves stretching them a bit further. It's pushing the comfort zone that's important, not recklessly and not without looking at the impact on others, but being creative with what you can do.

Being self-reliant is all about being self-driven amid chaos and uncertainty, while building career self-reliance means you will start to progress and use 'positioning' behaviours (i.e. career planning) to take advantage of new opportunities and even being more entrepreneurial in your thoughts about what you want to do. You need to combine your goal setting with a plan and work out the resources you need and who can help you get there.

4. Ambition and Networking

Do you consider yourself to be ambitious? Chances are yes, particularly as you are investing time in this book. Ambitious individuals create plans for their careers, looking ahead to where they move towards and research shows these individuals have higher resilience.

As you might expect, self-efficacy is a significant factor in driving ambition. As we will discuss further in Chapter 11, stretch opportunities at regular points in your career are essential to keep building on self-efficacy. The relationship between self-resilience and ambition is interdependent as both continue to feed into each other; higher self-resilience feeds into how we set goals. Let's just take a moment to think about ambitions in the context of discussions in this book. You may well be at crossroads in your career where you are considering the next steps in your current role or moving into a completely different field. A few important questions to consider: Who is in your line of vision? Who inspires you? Who are your role models? We asked you the question earlier in this book, what is your purpose? Who in your direct and even indirect network identifies different paths for you to become more adaptable in your career progression?

When we consider career shifts through emerging technology, we don't have a broad collection of inspirational role models as this whole area is so new in its development. So what's the solution? Well, the more creative you are in your thinking and the broader your network (and those in your line of vision), the easier it becomes for you to start making creative leaps for your career and even imagining new roles for yourself. If that sounds like a huge stretch and unimaginable, we have a small but impressive pipeline of new careers emerging.

5. Motivation to Learn

The study found that people who wanted to learn more and keep improving themselves also had high career resilience. This is such a good quality to have. Your formal education is over, but now is your learning time, into retirement and beyond. So, don't stop learning: keep your skills and mind fresh. Let life-long learning be your mantra.

The new world of work will, for sure, require you to learn new skills. You will also need to unlearn existing ones. As AI comes in and takes over routine jobs and makes some redundant, there will be new jobs and you will need to skill up. And it's also a resilient tool. By learning, you build your own value of yourself and your resilience grows. Become better aware of the learning and choices you need to make and ensure you always have the ability to learn new skills.

In this chapter we have mapped out the five areas of career resilience and as you reflect on these areas, you will recognize that none of them stand alone, but are in fact strands that come together to create a strong rope for your career progression. The next five chapters delve into specific areas of your leadership development, building on those areas to help you think about how you build your career resilience.

What does this model do for you?

Most importantly, the model shows that resilience is something we can develop in our practices and behaviours – they do work as the evidence showed they did. We know from literature discussed earlier in this chapter that developing your resilience will help in a number of ways as career-resilient people are more able to contribute to organizational growth and productivity by paying attention to their own career, thus giving a better performance.

It's important to reflect on all five aspects in the model but remember that career resilience underlines the importance of self-reliance. Career self-reliance is an essential quality in career management for entrepreneurial leaders as it requires individuals to remain open to opportunities and display flexibility in the management of their careers. And while we might think this is very 'modern new-age' thinking, in fact self-reliance has its early roots in essayists such as Ralph Waldo Emerson (1803–82), who wrote on the importance of self-reliance in his *Essays: First Series* in 1841. Emerson calls upon people to adopt a self-reliant attitude to enable more independent thought and take on more individualism, personal responsibility and nonconformity, as well as building on personal qualities: 'Be yourself; no base imitator of another, but your best self. There is something which you can do better than another. Listen to the inward voice and bravely obey that. Do the things at which you are great, not what you were never made for doing.'

Building your career resilience means not only are you being 'more you' but you are also developing your ability to self-manage. This is because building career resilience places an emphasis on 'bouncebackability leadership'. The essence of it for you means you'll develop a sense of greater agency over your career rather than reacting to what is given to you or what is immediately going on around you.

One of the most important things that we, as co-authors, want you to take away from the model and this chapter is to always maintain a learning mindset and to always (or at least regularly) create learning opportunities, as well as making and maintaining networks – more on this in Chapter 9. This means you will always be developing new skills (as appropriate to the market) and so have a more planned, rather than reactive, career approach. Ultimately, you'll be able to plan for future-of-work scenarios much better. In short, this model will make you stay employable for a long time.

CHAPTER SIX

Why cognitive diversity is necessary for successful leadership

Diversity in the workplace has become a business imperative to underpin improved innovation and financial business performance. Despite this recognition, there's no getting away from the reality – dealing with diversity is hard work, it's about fundamentally changing the culture of the organization, shifting to a new way of thinking and working. Every business depends on its workforce, their intellectual capital provides the basis of creativity and innovation that propel business performance.

The commitment to dig deeper and push harder has never been as evident as during the initial lockdown due to the pandemic. Across the world, organizations had to consider different ways of working and business as usual ceased. We have discussed the impact of the pandemic on careers in Chapter 4 (*see also* pp. 69–94), but what is evident is how organizations respond to the pandemic has a great deal to do with their internal resilience. The culture of institutions becomes hard-wired into the organization through policy, in particular that developed by HR to enshrine best practice. Other aspects of hard-wiring emerge from the industry of the organization – regulations, codes of conduct, as well as the wider legislative framework for the company. Behaviours and attitudes, often described as soft-wiring, make up the culture of the organization. We often assume changing behaviours and attitudes can be done more easily than addressing the 'harder' options, but in reality, both elements of hard- and soft-wiring create institutional barriers. Institutional barriers describe real and perceived blockers to changing the organization. Institutional barriers become embedded in the culture of the organization; they play an important role in creating internal stability so that resources are directed to performing in the market. Over the last decade, the swell of activity in the diversity and inclusion arena has demonstrated the rigidity of institutional barriers and how difficult it is to achieve behavioural change.

The diversity agenda is even more important in the context of emerging technology, as we introduced when describing the challenges of bias in programming in Chapter 3 (*see also* pp. 64–65). Building diverse teams is the way to address bias, but more importantly, creating a pluralistic culture mitigates for our proclivity to make decisions based on our biases. In this chapter we will address each of these areas as to why bias remains a problem and practically what can be done to mitigate for it; the value of cognitive diversity in teams and nurturing a culture where pluralism is encouraged and helps to challenge groupthink.

Bias and diversity in emerging tech

The lack of diverse experiences and perspectives reinforces biased attitudes and behaviours, particularly when decisions are made under pressure or when insufficient information is available. As we acknowledge the substantial impact of emerging tech on our working lives, it's important to peel back the cover and look at the composition of teams making decisions that affect every single one of us. In terms of subject matter, expertise and thought leadership, the inequities around diversity are stark. According to research by AI Now, only 18 per cent of authors at leading AI conferences are women and over 80 per cent of AI professors are men. The industry faces similar challenges: 'This disparity is extreme in the AI industry and women comprise only 15 per cent of AI research staff at Facebook and 10 per cent at Google. There is no public data on trans workers or other gender minorities. For black workers, the picture is even worse. For example, only 2.5 per cent of Google's workforce is black, while Facebook and Microsoft are each at 4 per cent. Given decades of concern and investment to redress this imbalance, the current state of the field is alarming.'[28]

Does this matter? Well, yes, because it would appear that many AI systems miss the nuanced, but important aspects of the user experience by women, people from different ethnic groups, trans and sexual orientation. If these elements are not programmed in, the level of inequity becomes hard-wired and more difficult to fix further down the road. When we consider some practical examples, we start to see the ramifications. Let's consider recruitment, where AI is increasingly used to filter applications. We know human recruitment includes unconscious bias and research consistently shows significant

---

[28]https://ainowinstitute.org/discriminatingsystems.pdf

unconscious bias against women, individuals from diverse ethnic backgrounds and older workers. Creating AI has the potential to remove unconscious human bias, but in order to do this, biases need to be identified and then weeded out. This is less about the programming capabilities and more about the rules on which decisions are made. What assumptions are factored into the algorithms? If programs are using the frameworks we have always used then the programming merely hard-wires our thinking. When things go wrong, they go spectacularly wrong and make strong headlines – for example, Amazon dropped its AI recruitment in 2018 when it was criticized for discriminating against women.[29]

Many commentators even offer warnings or dire consequences and use cases of AI causing harm and distress, such as in recruitment. As we discussed in Chapter 3 (*see also* pp. 47–67), facial recognition AI is seen as a boon for security in some areas, such as in banking and proving citizenship, but depending on who you are, it may have more sinister effects. Microsoft, Google and MIT all found that leading facial-recognition software packages performed poorly when identifying the gender of women and people of colour in comparison to its ability to classify male, white faces. In fact, the level of error was as high as 34.7 per cent for dark-skinned women compared to 0.8 per cent for light-skinned men.[30] Caroline Criado-Perez, author of *Invisible Women: Exposing Data Bias in a World Designed for Men*, identifies the impact of gender-based gaps in data on decisions that affect

---

[29]https://hbr.org/2019/10/using-ai-to-eliminate-bias-from-hiring
[30]https://news.mit.edu/2018/study-finds-gender-skin-type-bias-artificial-intelligence-systems-0212

everything from our health to mapping out city planning. In terms of AI, she admits the challenges are terrifying: 'We know that algorithms don't just reflect our biases back at us, they emphasize them significantly.' She goes on to explain the impact of groupthink: 'A homogeneous group will have gaps in their knowledge and that goes for ethnicity as well as gender as well as disability and all these different types of diversity.'[31]

As with any form of innovation, errors are an essential part of maturity but when the stakes are so high, it's easy to see why there have been calls to suspend or even ban some forms of facial-recognition software. Where are the boundaries? For example, in 2020, *Nature* magazine published an article debating the ethical issues around facial recognition in targeting oppressed minority groups. The article also cited the example of Harrisburg University in Pennsylvania in May 2020: researchers had developed facial recognition software to predict whether someone was going to be a criminal, and the AI had an 80 per cent accuracy rate and no racial bias.[32] It feels a bit like the movie, *Minority Report*, but worse because much of this perpetuates racial, gender and sexual orientation norms that are discriminatory and highly demeaning. A very influential social psychologist in the last century, Henri Tajfel, undertook experiments on social identity and social perceptions and found that humans identify groups and that leads to 'in-out' group thinking – which can lead to prejudice of the 'other' group. If now in this century we allow AI to create further in-out groups,

[31]https://www.digitalhealth.net/2020/02/caroline-criado-perez-rewired-2020
[32]https://www.nature.com/articles/d41586-020-03187-3

we can soon start seeing one group as lesser. It is therefore critical that we see AI as another social construct.

These examples illustrate the need for leaders to close the gap between emerging tech and every other area in the organization. Isabelle Borfiga, Innovation and Data Manager at MARCOL, explains the current challenges facing leaders in this area: 'There are two categories of people: the "pure" scientists and those who have to swim in the grey area of the data. The scientists will automatically default to a scientific method to output their expected result. They know what they're going to use, they know what the outcome is going to be, but they actually haven't taken the time to look at which information the raw data provides to make sure that everything will work accordingly. For any data project, it's essential to grasp what's going on with the data and then start testing your algorithms so that you can actually see that you've built something correctly. You see, in a business environment, different groups can get frustrated because the business leaders who don't have a scientific background might offer a different approach, but those who want to jump into the tech part won't necessarily want to follow business leaders' advice. However, in today's world, you can't have one without the other.'

Building cognitive diversity

Diversity is hard work because it requires us to change the way we do things and in most cases we have observed others to shape the way we work. When diversity is presented as a business case but also increasingly, intellectually, it is recognized as the way forward, but changing behaviour is incredibly testing and often where things get unstuck. Ask anyone who has taken on the challenge of doing something new and sticking to it: changing behaviour and attitude is difficult. We know all too well that for decades the health and fitness industry has spawned businesses working on the model of high aspirations but limited follow-through. Even when the change has a direct impact on our health, it's still incredibly hard to change. A research team from Italy examined the behaviour of patients who had been treated for acute coronary syndrome (for us mere mortals, understand this as being a heart attack). For patients, the benefits of medication to lower blood pressure or cholesterol could also be achieved by quitting smoking. Relapse is acknowledged as a serious challenge for patients but in this case by the end of the first year, a staggering 63 per cent of patients had started smoking again. Even more alarming, within this group of patients who relapsed, half had begun smoking within 20 days of leaving the hospital.[33]

Even when making change can radically alter the quality of our life, it is clearly still incredibly difficult to make the necessary changes, so what hope do we have for organizations addressing institutional barriers? Well, for the 47 per cent of people who did not resume smoking, their chances of improved life expectancy and quality of life would have improved considerably. We are drawn to such individuals, who challenge the norm and break patterns, because we recognize the willpower it has taken to get there. As we will discuss, grit underpins this success.

---

[33]https://uk.reuters.com/article/us-smoking/return-to-smoking-after-heart-attack-ups-death-risk-idUSTRE76L2ZP20110722

However, on the flip side, work by Angela Duckworth, Professor of Psychology at the University of Pennsylvania and author of *Grit*, shows that we can also generate negative reactions to people who excel as a result of hard work, particularly when the example forces us to consider our own shortcomings and lack of commitment to work hard or see through a project. In her book, *Grit*, she cites the example of research measuring attitudes towards concert pianists who were considered to be born with the talent to excel in music. As individuals realized it was not completely pure talent but actually involved significant investment of time spent practising, the adulation around the performers diminished.

Duckworth explains that the shift in attitude has everything to do with how we respond to success in others based on our expectations: if we are convinced we have the tools in hand to make changes, the opportunities are boundless. More work is unfolding in this area through Stanford Professor Carol Dweck's work on the growth mindset, focusing on academic performance of schoolchildren.[34] We reach a point where we recognize that yes, change is hard work, it takes effort, commitment and perseverance, but we know change can happen and for those who achieve it, the rewards can literally be life-changing. For organizations to reap the rewards of diversity initiatives, the view needs to be incremental and long term, as explained by Deborah Richards: 'We need to do things differently in order not to recreate the same mistakes or the same challenges in 10

---

[34]https://www.ted.com/speakers/carol_dweck

years' time with the gender agenda. How do we actually create that ripple effect? If we consider gender and ethnicity, this is such a challenging issue. I mean, for example, our gender data has still stayed the same. We have not changed. We have not moved the needle despite recruiting 50:50 men and women. We have not moved the needle. And that is because women have to select themselves into the workplace quite often. I am passionate about intersectionality because no one fits in one box, but what I'm really also passionate about is removing those barriers and finding people who will absolutely stand up and help people sponsor people to really fulfil their potential.'

Jeff Phipps, Managing Director UK & Ireland at ADP, explains why change is hard work: 'How do I change the behaviours of people like me? I want to be really careful when I'm asked "what's your advice to well-intended men, and for women?". I think you've got to quickly figure out your place in any organization. Most organizations are trying to fight their way through that and there are probably some, you know, there are probably some out there that just, you know, are not really taking the things seriously when it comes to diversity in all its forms. I think it's a very personal decision, that you have to come to determine how you feel about that organization and if it's not one that's in a position where you genuinely feel it accepts you for who you are, what's your role in changing what you fight for? If you find yourself in an organization you love and it's accepting you for who you are, and you're happy there, then that's a great thing, and I hope that you realize that organization that has genuinely worked hard to deliver that, but probably had to work quite hard to get there.'

This viewpoint is the crux of the diversity agenda: yes, it's hard work and no, it's not a sheep dip or a fair-weather agenda. But before we get caught in the weeds of diversity, let's review the evidence that provides the business case and remember that while diversity is about creating better working experiences for everyone, because change is such hard work we need to be extremely clear about the benefits.

Innovation is one of our core themes throughout this book and an increasingly important area of focus for organizations. Accenture shows innovation is the third most important leadership priority. Their research revealed that 57 per cent of leadership thought that innovation was important (covering services, products and content) in third place to financial performance (76 per cent) and brand or quality (72 per cent). In fast-changing markets, financial performance and brand and quality are heavily intertwined with innovation. In the same report, just over a third of leaders (34 per cent) prioritized diversity. Different metrics demonstrated the revenue potential of diversity; the Accenture report identifies that global profits would be 33 per cent per cent higher (equivalent to $3.7 trillion in 2019) as a result of staff from minority backgrounds feeling more included and therefore more 'productive' in their organizations.[35]

The direct impact on creating an innovation mindset and demonstrating a 10 per cent increase would result in global

---

[35]https://www.accenture.com/_acnmedia/Thought-Leadership-Assets/PDF-2/Accenture-Getting-To-Equal-2020-Research-Report.pdf

GDP increasing by up to $8 trillion by 2028. The companies lagging behind would see staff engagement six times lower than their competitors and counterparts who embed diversity into their DNA. In their review on the performance between diversity and innovation, McKinsey launched the results of their findings from a dataset of 15 countries and over 1,000 companies.[36] The survey builds on the data from previous surveys in 2017 and 2014 and the results make for interesting analysis of the situation.

The 2019 report showed companies in the top quartile for gender diversity on executive teams were 25 per cent more likely to have above-average profitability than those in the bottom quartile. The performance of those companies had significantly increased from 15 per cent in 2014 to 21 per cent in 2017. This trend demonstrates how value accumulates as the benefits of gender diversity are embedded in the culture of the organization. Before we finish this section, a further piece of evidence from the McKinsey report: the notion of 'one then done', the idea that having one woman in executive leadership is sufficient progress. McKinsey found that companies with more than 30 per cent female executives were more likely to outperform other companies; within the range of 10–30 per cent, the companies they outperformed had less than 30 per cent female executives or none at all.

Building an evidence base for diversity requires certain groups to be identified as the basis for measurements. In most countries, gender is still the dominant metric for

---

[36]https://www.mckinsey.com/featured-insights/diversity-and-inclusion/diversity-wins-how-inclusion-matters

diversity as 50 per cent of the world's population is female.[37] There are a number of other important characteristics that are recognized in different countries – race and ethnicity, sexual orientation, socio-economic background, disability, even age. Most people will sit across two or more groups, leading to increased focus on the idea of intersectionality. Over time, we will see more data based on the different sub-groups, with further correlations between diversity and performance, but suffice to say the focus has shifted away from why diversity matters to how do we harness the value of diversity in teams and across organizations? Tamara Box, Managing Partner EME at legal firm Reed Smith explains how minority groups may be better placed to build a new form of leadership: 'Relational leadership may, in fact, be even easier for minority groups, as people who have been marginalized probably understand the value of relationships even more than those for whom power has come with privilege. For too many years, groupthink has caused companies to replicate traditional leadership with more of the same, believing that what has worked in the past will work in the future. So the short answer is yes, qualities, skills, and mindsets differ for people from minority groups. And that is exactly why we need them in our organizations and in our leadership. Diversity, another word for "difference," sparks innovation, drives equality, improves profitability, and creates broader opportunities for every individual and company. People with different qualities, skills, and mindsets are the stars that

---

[37]https://www.mckinsey.com/featured-insights/diversity-and-inclusion/diversity-wins-how-inclusion-matters

can make our companies shine, but we won't benefit if we don't get them onto centre stage.'

If we accept that innovation requires diversity and there's no way around it, then the emphasis is on how leaders create terms to allow diversity to flourish. The default for this approach in the diversity field is to create inclusive leadership. Fundamentally, there is a challenge with this approach. The word itself is a Latin word, *inclure*, which means 'to enclose'. Think about what that means: we work extremely hard to recruit a diverse group of candidates into a department and then during the onboarding process, we wring out all the valuable differences to ensure they think like one of us; at best, we may tolerate differences. Tolerate doesn't quite have the same ring as celebrating difference. Do you remember a time when you were tolerated? That experience didn't do much for your enthusiasm or even your confidence. Chances are, you weren't bringing your best self to the table and you were certainly not brimming with creativity and innovative thinking. So, what's the alternative? Well, in a phase of pivoting, it's time for the diversity to follow suit – we need to start talking about pluralistic leadership. Pluralism is rooted in the notion that differences of experiences and perspectives are to be welcomed, encouraged and celebrated. Actively engaging with different perspectives requires a willingness to learn, to develop genuine curiosity in your colleagues, and to recognize that you don't have all the answers but you may need to let go of certain social biases that stop you from engaging.

Miranda Zhao, Risk Analytics Managing Director at Lloyds Banking Group explains that the power of questions helps to open up conversations but also steer dialogue into new areas; But that is only the first step in planting a seed. 'Asking questions is easy, but then once you've asked the question, most people will have to create the bandwidth, think about solution. Then the next time when they come back, they're prepped to engage. And that for me is important, because everyone has their own agenda to solve, and you have your agenda to solve. So it is your duty to help raise awareness by starting to ask questions.'

Some people may argue that creating diversity in the team is enough and the culture of the team will allow for differences to bubble up to the surface. Well, groupthink is a far stronger barrier to the idea of diversity organically influencing and shaping the culture. We will spend time later in this chapter discussing groupthink and some practical ways you can manage it.

Creating pluralistic cultures in teams and organizations

A pluralistic culture is based on building the strength of teams valuing the diversity of experiences and thinking in coming up with solutions, creating the conditions for cognitive diversity. The real value from diversity emerges through cognitive diversity; delving deeper into the richness of experiences, socialized learning, perspectives. Cognitive diversity is a term we need to spend more time developing and understanding and we will come back to it and provide a slightly deeper dive further on in this chapter. As organizations become more dispersed and leadership more distributed (*see also* Chapter 4), teams have the opportunity to flex their perspective and approaches to build a more comprehensive approach to understanding complex problems. This is a lot to think about, but here's a perspective: if we think about developing inclusive leadership in relationship to specific groups – for example, gender, race or sexuality – what happens as new sub-groups emerge or the intersectionality debate becomes even stronger? If we expect leaders to keep learning new ways of leading and adapting to whichever group is the latest priority, fatigue will set in very quickly. Fatigue is often quickly followed by surrender and momentum and the benefits through change evaporate. Adopting a pluralistic approach allows leaders to develop a leadership style that is constantly open and welcoming and in doing so, accessible to all team members, irrespective of whether or not they sit in one or many diversity targets or indeed in none at all.

Meredith Preston McGhie, Secretary General of the Global Centre for Pluralism, based in Ottawa, Canada, states that pluralism is at its heart an ethic of respect for diversity. 'Diversity becomes the basis for more successful and prosperous societies (and organizations) and not something to be managed and overcome. At the same time, we must recognize that tolerance and inclusion are only a part of the necessary transformation process for a pluralistic society.'[38]

A pluralistic culture creates the conditions for creativity and innovation to become embedded in the DNA of a team. Cognitive diversity goes far beyond the surface to use the common iceberg analogy when discussing diversity and

---

[38]https://www.pluralism.ca/press-release/meredith-preston-mcghie-on-going-beyond-tolerance-and-inclusivity/

gets to the centre of our thinking. Each of us has a rich and unique perspective on the world and, in the words of author, Max Tegmark, author of *Life 3.0*, this is what makes and keeps us human. As we will discuss in Chapter 9 on learning, formal learning in the earlier stages of childhood is predetermined by parents, carers and society in terms of what constitutes a strong foundation. Research shows how education practices can create homogeneity in classrooms with overarching beliefs and attitudes, sometimes based on gender stereotypes – boys don't play with dolls, girls don't play with cars (The Global Centre for Pluralism has launched an ambitious plan to introduce pluralistic thinking into schools, shaping thinking around leadership education across academic and essential professional services staff).

If you think back to your childhood, teenage years, early adulthood, which are the periods when you felt the greatest need to conform? The stimulus can come from different sources: peer pressure at school or friends in communities, parental expectations, wider cultural and community norms, platforms through social media? At a time when identities become more fluid and changing trends move faster than ever, finding safety with a peer group creates the emotional need to stay comfortable. The paradox is that despite access to the widest amount of information, data and opinions to stay within the groups we are comfortable with, we will find ways to blunt those jagged edges.

Matthew Syed, author, journalist and former Olympic table-tennis player, explains how we become used to tuning out thoughts or ideas that challenge our thinking and the implications when groups made up of highly intelligent people reinforce homophily through recruitment and subsequently thinking.[39] His book, *Rebel Ideas*, is filled with numerous examples of how groupthink has had a substantial impact on our lives. One example that illustrates the impact of perspective blindness in the business world is a piece of research led by two academics from the University of Michigan: Richard E. Nisbett and Takahiko Masuda. The experiment identified two groups: the first group consisted of Americans and the second group of Japanese. Both groups watched video clips of underwater scenes, filled with sea life and brimming with activity. When asked to provide feedback on what they saw, there was a significant difference reported between the two groups. The American group described the variety of fish and sealife in great detail, even focusing on the patterns and colours of the different fish and the size of the groups. In contrast, the Japanese group focused on the background and the context, the nature of the water and the landscape underwater. Interestingly, the focus on the fish was viewed as a side comment. Syed describes the outcome: 'It was as if the group were seeing different scenes, shaped by differences in culture. America is a more individualistic society; Japanese culture is more interdependent. Americans tend to focus on objects; Japanese on context'. Digging deeper with this experiment illustrates that systematic differences being shaped by culture create different frames of reference in relation to observing and experiencing the world. This perspective blindness does not imply a lack of

---

[39]Syed, M. (2020) *Rebel Ideas, the power of diverse thinking*. United Kingdom: John Murray Publishers Ltd.

intelligence – in fact, far from it – but if a team thinks in the same way, how are they prepared to handle the 'wicked problems' we face? As previously discussed, these complex challenges do not have a blueprint to provide a 'cut and paste' approach, albeit with incremental adjustments.

Let's begin with what's going on inside our brains, our most complex and hugely efficient organ. It is estimated that we make somewhere in the region of 35,000 conscious and subconscious decisions daily[40]; the number may be far higher and we're not even factoring in the unconscious decisions. Think about what decisions you made in the first hour after waking up this morning. Take a moment to consider this: did you debate whether or not to get out of bed, whether to brush your teeth, what to listen to … the list is endless. Perhaps the easiest recollection of decision making this morning was what you planned to wear or eat for breakfast (if that's your habit). If you note down how many decisions you made in the few hours after waking up – the conscious and subconscious decisions – your list will be anywhere from a few hundred to a few thousand. Imagine what would transpire if you continued this exercise every few hours in the day. That list could very quickly fill a notebook.

Why is this discussion important? It reminds us of how busy our brain is and the level of work required of it every 24 hours. In terms of calorific intake, our brains can consume anywhere from 25 to 40 per cent per cent of our daily intake. Higher intake is correlated with working harder – for example, learning

---

[40]Sahakian, B. & LaBuzetta, J.N. (2013) *Bad Moves: How decision making goes wrong and the ethics of smart drugs.* London: Oxford University Press.

new skills or conditions of stress where we need to think with more effort. If we stopped to think about the decisions we have to make, we would literally become paralyzed with the raft of them. In order for us to function, our brains need to work effectively and allow us to invest attention in the more challenging areas. An important by-product of our efficient brains is biased behaviour: when faced with new situations or meeting new people, we will scan through our memories in milliseconds to determine whether the new experience presents a threat or is safe. As we navigate through a greater understanding of biased behaviour, we know socialization plays an essential element in shaping our biases.

To benefit from cognitive diversity, leaders need to recognize the institutional barriers to be addressed. The leadership lens and experience on diversity is very different to what happens across the wider organization; returning to the research by Accenture, a fifth of employees feel they are not welcome and can't contribute to their organization. Sixty-eight per cent of leadership feel they are creating empowering environments but only a third of employees agree with this perspective. Belonging to an ingroup is central to our sense of existing – without it, we feel vulnerability, a threat to our existence.

While this can seem far-fetched, the implications are real and can impact whether we flourish or flounder at work. Consider the last time you joined a new team: as you acclimatized, you spent time getting to understand the dynamics, the powerbase, the culture of the team, how communication was handled. How long was it before you challenged the voice of senior colleagues, how comfortable did you feel before you thought you could take an opposing stance and feel safe or valued? What happens when there is a discussion with your team (and you are not the most senior person), what are you likely to do? You may look around at your colleagues and gauge their reactions. Of course you may decide to speak out, but if you don't, you spend time trying to understand the perspective of and possibly even align your thinking with the majority. If you are in the minority for whatever basis – demographic (gender, ethnicity, age) or your knowledge base and perspective – you are less likely to speak out and voice an opposing view as you won't have other members backing you up. This is the basis of groupthink: if we are socialized into respecting hierarchies and leadership and our value is correlated with being a good team player (in other words, well-behaved and compliant), then it's far harder to break the team culture and challenge thinking. Creating openness relies heavily on the culture set by leadership and this means going beyond paying lip service to proactively encouraging different views. Some companies call this 'obligation to dissent' as an expected behaviour drilled into new recruits during the onboarding process. Creating a culture where constructively challenging suggestions and the way things are done needs explicit permission, consistently.

Creating a culture where dissent is encouraged is the bedrock of creativity and innovation, but this needs a conscious approach to culture, as explained by Richard Dickson, COO and President of Mattel, Inc.:

'You have to give permission to be creative, to be stimulated by a groupthink, and to come up with innovative solutions to some of the problems the world is facing. As a lead, it's about being brave enough to act on the ideas. Sometimes you can overthink a decision. There are consensus leaders and there are conviction leaders. You have got to make early decisions on what to do and what not to do – in that you have choices of decisions where you can apply your own value set, such as saying a particular client has a set of values so far against yours and that of the company, you feel you don't want to work with them. And in many cases, you could miss an opportunity because you don't have the strength of your own conviction. There needs to be a careful balance between being overly aggressive and being, you know, fundamentally responsible, but that is where I believe a fine line can make or break a leader and a company. We know that risk doesn't just happen, you don't just magic it up overnight, it's a learned skill and your tolerance for risk in your ability to trust your instinct and learn from failure. So again, it's not something you can just do, if you've played it safe your whole life. You can't suddenly transform into a risk taker. And if you step into leadership, you don't automatically wear that cloak of risk. You have to be incredibly conscious as a leader of everything that's happening around you. And I believe that that is the type of courage and conviction leaders need to have to be able to bring your best and brightest into a room, put forth a challenge, and have creative dialogue and imagine what could be possible, and then ultimately be brave enough to act on those ideas, you know, to drive the creative idea through is really what creative actually is.'

The most critical element is ensuring leaders actually walk the talk, by showing vulnerability and an openness to thinking about new ideas and acknowledging the input of new ideas in shaping suggestions. As with anything that requires behavioural change, while the sentiment is welcomed, it can be very hard work to achieve this mindset shift. It can be very hard work to achieve this mindset shift. To change organizational culture means regulating the external emotions within the internal culture, and at times these two areas will be incongruent.

All organizations have goals that emerge from a combination of big vision and desire to fulfil a specific need. In some cases there was probably some artistry in dreaming and designing a vision for an organization. As it became a reality the vision had to meet many outcomes, not least the goals of growth, efficiency, innovation and improvement – which are all geared around measuring performance. And because these goals are visible deliverables, you, as a leader, can make your impact. Then you can start widening the goals of performance and measure the valuable impact.

CHAPTER SEVEN

Getting comfortable with data-driven leadership

Data leadership is an increasingly important leadership skill. When we look at organizations, it is clear to see the gulf between leaders and data scientists, each working in their silos. The separation of thinking and application in these areas has enormous ramifications when it comes to developing and programming in AI and emerging technology. Strategic decisions and outcomes mean well-sourced data and analysis are necessary. As Daniel Hulme, CEO of Satalia, said: 'With machine learning, data science and statistics are great at finding patterns in data, but the most important thing is making decisions that leverage the patterns found in data. This requires a completely different set of skills: discrete mathematics, operations research and optimization. These skills are massively underrepresented in industry.'

The essential qualities of leaders require a better understanding of the critical nature of data, from inception to planning to collection and analysis. The impact of improved technology capabilities means we have access to far more data than ever before and the potential is immense, so much so that data is described as the new oil. Sathya Bala, Head of Global Data Governance at a luxury goods company, explains the integral nature of data to leadership decisions: 'Data cannot be separated from our work life, what we do and how we do it. We need to ensure all our colleagues see data not as a fringe thing or an IT/techy thing, but something we all deal with and a key tool in business and a key ingredient to how we analyze, communicate and make decisions.' She goes on to explain how leaders must develop the capabilities to become more comfortable handling data: 'We need to ensure our leaders are talking about data and role-modelling good data practices. Emerging leaders should get comfortable with data, understand how it relates to their role, but also how data underpins the key processes and outcomes of the organization. All leaders of the future will need to learn and continue to stay up to date on the role of data in business and society. You do not need to be an expert, but you need to be aware of the changing landscape of business and data is part of that change. It is part of building your commercial acumen – just as you would read up about digital developments in your industry, you should do the same with data.'

As an entrepreneurial leader you need to become more comfortable about breaking new ground in decision making, but to do this effectively, you need to mitigate risk. Entrepreneurs are not random risk takers, but take calculated risks when innovating and creating new initiatives. Instinct is an important element of decision making, but even more important is the ability to spot trends from data and belief in your experience and expertise. Becoming more comfortable with data allows you to make decisions on the basis of calculated risk (more on this later in the chapter). Breaking down the key elements of understanding data, we cover the following areas in this chapter: demystifying data, handling the challenges of data, and data-driven leadership.

Demystifying data for leadership

The notion of data being the new oil originated in 2005 and is attributed to British mathematician and entrepreneur Clive Humby OBE, but it was revived in a report published by the *Economist* in 2017: 'The world's most valuable resource is no longer oil, but data'[41]. Within the tech sector, business models are flourishing where the data is the dominant commodity; we only have to consider our willingness to use email accounts or access information for 'free'. A free service means we are not paying, but we are certainly trading our information and data to help online providers build up patterns and trends based on our behaviour.

As a result, data is becoming embedded across different functions. Consider, for example, the impact of marketing, as shared by Leila Ratnani, EMEA Lead Channel Strategist, Facebook: 'Marketing, in the old school mentality, started out that way – the big talk, the "fluffiness", the deals being made down over lunch – primarily in the print and TV world. I started my career in search advertising and of course we can start with what we might think are the terms people search for in our grandiose opinion of ourselves (speaking from a client perspective), however it is then the data and numbers that started to drive decisions and optimizations.

---

[41]Humby, C. (2017) 'The world's most valuable resource is no longer oil, but data'. *The Economist*, 6th May https://www.economist.com/leaders/2017/05/06/the-worlds-most-valuable-resource-is-no-longer-oil-but-data

At that time, search was a bit more sophisticated than pure digital media, which was basically a bunch of companies who went out and bought remnant inventory for cheap and ran traffic to clients' sites and as a numbers game, it looked great and clients were happy but in the digital space, that was never going to be enough and we now consider the true data that we can extract from digital media and the behaviours we can learn from what we are seeing to better engage with our audience.'

To get specific about the channels of data, there are a number of sources where you provide vast amounts of intelligence:

- The sites you visit; the time and length of time you spend at each site;
- A pattern in the types of sites you visit (for example, sports, news health, fashion and so on), allowing social media companies to generate audience profiles;
- The types of ad you engage with – whether you hover, click or ignore;
- Your behaviour after engagement;
- Your reactions to messages, images, even colours.

Ratnani goes on to explain the shift in the marketing approach: 'We are starting to look at marketing [through] a much more scientific lens, requiring the switch in how laws are applied to cases to what the data is showing us, and how we can learn from it to make things better and stronger in terms of delivery and engagement. Digital media has progressed one step further to a "programmatic" model – now where it gets interesting with AI and Automation. In this world, systems can be programmed to find the people we want to reach (based on the data segments above) and, where necessary, additional data sets can be purchased. Data is now king and is taken much more notice of, even by clients themselves who hold a number of data points on their customers. Data is not an evil king but one that can make human experiences and engagements more engaging and relevant. The digital sphere is much more complex and the rules are constantly changing, based on human behaviour. In my mind, the data and the human aspect are still connected as you cannot fully understand this new world without having experienced and understood the data. The "fluffy" approach that dominated these decisions previously would now get you laughed out of the building with most clients. The skill comes in identifying those just starting their digital adventure and then knowing how to bring them on your learning journey to get them on board with the digital landscape.'

When discussing data, it is easy to zoom in on a specific area and more often than not the practical elements – for example, how the data is collected and first-level analysis. The essential elements start at the inception: what questions are you asking and for what purpose? Having tonnes of data in itself is not the solution, the real value occurs in how the data collection is constructed and how the results are disseminated.

Data is emerging as a function in companies with an increase in data governance roles but equally essential is the development of a data strategy that is aligned to short-, medium- and long-term goals. In the wider business sense, when we deal with emerging tech we can get confused or mesmerized by terms such as 'deep learning' or 'machine learning'. These algorithms can seem to offer robust solutions and, as we discussed in Chapter 3, there are overwhelming benefits to these technologies. In order to identify trends, particularly when you are not entirely sure what you are looking for, the quality of data is paramount. In Chapter 6, we discussed the challenges faced when AI is based on incomplete data sets (*see also* pp. 118–122) and for the most part, the conversation on data sets has focused on gender and racial diversity. AI libraries need to become more robust but in order to do this, the criteria for inclusion need to cover the widest possible data sets yet still manage to be pragmatic and sufficient to generate statistically valid results. AI requires substantial datasets and this is pushing the data model adopted by so many tech firms. Unlike oil, which is finite, humans can produce millions of data points for as long they exist and engage with tech. The argument for data gathering at scale by companies is that large data sets are needed for their machine-learning AI models and this is so that they can fine-tune a better, more personalized offer based on our behavioural data – which we like.

Working in the diversity arena for the last decade, we have seen a noticeable step change in the use of data-driven and evidence-based approaches towards impactful diversity initiatives. While this is a significantly positive step change in behaviour, there is also a risk that people can talk about data without properly interrogating its integrity. As this field is still evolving, the most important role you have is to ask questions: why the data is being collected, what it's being used for and how it will impact strategic decision making for your teams and organization.

Michael Swaisland, Head of Insights EMEA, Mattel, Inc., explains the necessity to be conscious about data-driven leadership: 'We are all swimming in data, but driving action from it becomes more of a challenge, the more you collect. We need to be able to cut through the noise so that people can more easily digest and act. Within insights, this is leading to focus across the board on automation, removal of data silos and leaving reporting to software and using people to think, challenge, discuss and drive for new opportunities.' He reinforces the same message from everyone we spoke to about this area: software can report, but human intellect and creativity is fundamental for decision making.

We will come back to creativity and its role in leadership in Chapter 9 when we talk about learning and leadership resources, but the big takeaway from this discussion is to ensure you are comfortable with asking fundamental questions about data because over time others will expect you to have core data competences in your decision making.

Oily data slips away

If we continue with the data-as-oil analogy, then we know the real value emerges when oil is refined. Just as with oil, data in its raw state doesn't easily lend itself to emerging trends and opportunities. What becomes equally important is not just understanding the data but building a narrative around it, to help others make sense of patterns and see the opportunities you have spotted. Think back to the first quarter of 2020: with the exception of China, almost every country was beginning to hear stories about a virus, but as it was new and unproven and on the whole, people hadn't heard about it, they refused to accept this could be a threat. We don't have to exert a great deal of imagination to consider the ridiculousness of that statement and these initial reactions when we now consider how the virus has radically altered our way of living. We only need to think about the impact in non-food retail to understand how companies reacted so differently in response to the disruption during the initial stages of the pandemic. How did online retailer ASOS experience a 329 per cent increase in profits, while the largest department chain in the UK, Debenhams, and global retailer Arcadia both collapsed, leading to the loss of 25,000 jobs in the UK alone?

According to Walter Loeb, Forbes contributor and senior retail analyst, the list of retail store closures across the US is overwhelming.[42] The list of companies highlights the disparity in performance between traditional high-street retailers compared with online companies, the latter having built their business model around data, underpinning speed of delivery and convenience. Retail businesses built around traditional models found it more challenging to adjust to shifts in stock demands (fewer suits, ties and work shoes, more activewear, home office and consumer electronics). According to Google Insights, in the UK in 2019, 41 per cent of fashion purchases were online and 59 per cent were

---

[42]https://www.forbes.com/sites/walterloeb/2020/07/06/9274-stores-are-closing-in-2020-its-the-pandemic-and-high-debt-more-will-close/?sh=1cfc5524729f

offline; in 2020, online fashion purchases sky-rocketed to 86 per cent and offline was a paltry 14 per cent.[43] Traditional retailers were not equipped to react to the exogenous shocks they experienced; as the data did not transfer to planning, retailers saw shortages in products from masks and visors to essential food items and even toilet rolls in certain countries.

Beyond the impact of data in the retail sector, we also saw major upheavals in the health provision for individuals impacted by COVID-19. In the UK and US, when the data was analyzed on the basis of ethnicity, huge disparities emerged, particularly in terms of survival rates. Individuals from black and Asian ethnic backgrounds experienced higher death rates, leading to an outcry about the level of support available for these groups. Further analysis identified a raft of reasons – correlating results with lifestyle factors, types of jobs (a disproportionate number of frontline healthcare professionals in lower-skilled roles come from these ethnic groups) and housing conditions – extended families living together. At a macro level, national comparisons around COVID-19 were equally challenging as countries recorded and reported on data using different metrics, making it even more difficult to provide comparable baselines. Even with a global pandemic, countries were unable to provide a unified approach to collecting, presenting and comparing data to help the public make sense of what was occurring nationally and globally.

---

[43]https://www.thinkwithgoogle.com/intl/en-gb/consumer-insights/consumer-trends/consumers-adapted-shopping-behaviour-covid

In a further twist, we also witnessed the backlash through the abuse of data generated from 'track and trace'. The UK was not alone in creating a track and trace app, but through the process of implementation, Serco – the company contracted to deliver track and trace – stumbled on a series of mishaps through inadequate training, detailing the information of recruits and using social media inappropriately to help them complete details of COVID-19, all of which underpin examples of data breaches. Furthermore, problems occurred when businesses were found to be using track and trace data for marketing.

Reactions to these examples demonstrate the complexity of ethics and data. It seems strange to bring complexity into this argument, but as these three very different examples demonstrate, our reactions to retailers not being responsive enough to our stock demands are more minor than the anger felt for certain ethnic groups being exposed to the virus and risking their lives to keep earning.

The use of data from track and trace is an area likely to create far more disparity in the range of reactions. We can understand this better if we consider data through the lens of digital natives, as described by Katrina Pugh, lecturer at Columbia University and President, AlignConsulting, who says: 'They [digital natives] grew up on Google and Wikipedia, with millions of answers, generously (or passively) crowdsourced, just ripe for the taking. But, when it comes to data being "free", they have a nuanced view. If taxpayer money pays for data, it should be open, they argue. "Free" has limits. Digital Natives respect the work involved in telling a story from data. This new generation learns about data acquisition, artificial intelligence and information visualization in school. Notably, many are aware of the heavy lift involved with data collection and preparation. They are concerned that there is too much "free" data on social media. They read rants and are sceptical that they're being manipulated. They worry about how people are forming opinions from opinions – the blight of social media – without "good" research. What's dangerous, however, is Digital Natives' faith that data-volume will shake down the truth. For most, search trumps navigating, and there is a belief that metadata will arise out of natural language processing engines. The issue is proportion: most organizations, even big ones, are meaning-rich and data-poor, so supervising collaboration, curation and search is non-negotiable.'

As this discussion demonstrates, data is complex and it's important to have a comfortable grip to know how it works and how you can build greater comfort in handling data in your decision making. These examples show how data has rippled through economic, social and legal issues and has the potential to create huge ruptures in how we behave and make decisions as societies. Equally important is how colleagues around us and the wider public react and respond to how organizations use their data. What is acceptable to you may be completely unacceptable to one of your closest friends or colleagues. Depending on our level of digital comfort, we will have very different levels of tolerance towards when our data is used and for what purpose.

The challenge for leaders is navigating the delicate balance between utilizing data and bringing creative thinking into new decisions. If every decision, and in particular, the big decisions dealing with 'wicked problems', is driven solely by data, the inevitable risk is diminishing the impact of creativity leading to genuinely new ideas. Richard Foster-Fletcher of NeuralPath.io highlights the challenge: 'As a leader, you cannot say "in data we trust" and then hope that out-of-box thinking will thrive in your organization. Whilst Google's core revenues came from harnessing their massive data sets to deliver best in class page rankings and targeted ads, some of their most innovative products came from the mandated new ideas time (20 per cent of the week) – for example, products such as Gmail, Google Sunroof, AdSense and Google News.'

Getting to grips with data, with emerging technology, in addition to knowing your market well are the fundamental principles for leadership, as explained by Sir John Chisholm: 'If you understand how to access data and you have an understanding of fundamental tools, AI and all the rest of the zillion ways in which those tools can be applied, you have the potential to make real transformational changes in all sorts of spaces. If you are working in a large organization, people who are not up to speed and don't necessarily understand the use of technology or data in the same way as you won't understand the potential. This is definitely an issue with data but it's only really useful once you apply it to something which really needs it. It is beguiling to get in to say "hey, look what I can find here". It's about getting a lot deeper rather than getting caught up in the superficial elements, but actually really questioning and questioning the application and the value of new opportunities.'

Doing the right data leadership

If we look back at the sparks that created innovations in previous industrial revolutions, we saw Henry Ford's fantastic innovation of the Ford motorcar. An apocryphal quote attributed to him is this: 'If I had asked people what they wanted, they would have said faster horses.' If we consider the quote in the current context of decision making there is a very strong chance we wouldn't have the automobile industry as we know it. Imagine if Ford went down the data science route: he wouldn't have developed something that customers at that time would not have imagined they wanted or needed. It is something all emerging leaders also need to consider – innovations may not come from your data. Adaptations (such as to a more diverse customer group) may not be in your data sets. Nuances you need to develop your product and service may not be seen because your customers didn't a) have a voice, b) were not able to articulate needs, and c) didn't even know what was possible! As emerging leaders, pay attention to the unexpected and the unknown. Research by Naeema in her doctoral study showed that those people who are open to new experience and ideas *and* are good at analyzing can manage uncertainty better – and even did better out of it (Pasha, 2020). So, don't just look to be data led, become data intelligent.

Building a strong narrative around data is equally important when it comes to building confidence in data intelligence.

Data is largely objective and rationalized and while this is important in trusting the integrity of data, it doesn't mean we are willing to engage with the findings, especially when the results seem so far-fetched we can't relate to them. We only have to consider the impact on retailing discussed earlier in this chapter to see the consequences of not being able to comprehend and make timely decisions around the data. This is where your value as a leader becomes critical as you build a story to demonstrate what the data is showing.

Any good storyteller will remind you the core to an impactful story lies in creating emotional connections – hooks for recipients to access abstract ideas and develop confidence in understanding the key elements. This in turn helps your colleagues to contribute to problem-solving, bringing together immense value from the data and creating practical and successful solutions. Charismatic leadership recognizes the immense value of stories to envelop and create emotional connections with colleagues and have powerful effects in moving listeners into a different headspace.

Rachel Higham, Chief Information Officer at WPP, sees the role of data and information officers as essential in changing the way we think and make decisions: 'As we embrace new technologies and working practices, many require a shift in culture, mindset and behaviours. So a CIO has to be able to lead cultural change to support colleagues in abandoning silos, to embrace cross functional working, to prototype and iterate their way to solutions, and to focus not on deploying technology, but on driving adoption and shifts in outcomes and experiences. Typically 90 per cent of an organization's data is disconnected and inaccessible. Curating and surfacing data to provide insight and improve decision making across the organization is essential. We need to move towards an insight driven culture through the organization.'

When thinking about building entrepreneurial leadership capabilities with a strong data-driven leadership, this framework may help you to think about the key areas and where you need to pay attention, particularly as you read the next few chapters about your own leadership development:

This model for entrepreneurial leadership builds on our traditional understanding of leadership capabilities by augmenting the need to have more confidence handling data – as we have discussed in this chapter – and merging this with greater confidence in creative thinking capabilities, which we will discuss further in Chapter 8. The sweet spot is the middle, where you have sufficient confidence in how to apply data and creative thinking to your decision making in a manner such that it becomes an integral component of your leadership.

As you reflect on this model, it may be useful to ask yourself the following questions to help you identify where you need to pay more attention for your own leadership development:

- How comfortable are you about having regular conversations with data experts as part of your routine decision making?
- How often do you question data presented to you?
- How do you consider the story emerging from the data and how you present this narrative to the most critical colleagues in your group?

If you have answered any of these questions with uncertainty, then data is still not a key skill for your entrepreneurial capabilities. There are similar questions around creativity that we will address in the next chapter.

CHAPTER EIGHT

Career dynamism: the tools you need for your career

By now, you are very comfortable with the notion of the need for career reinvention or re-imagination and taking a resilient, entrepreneurial approach to your career development. The significant challenge is recognizing that while you are changing, the wider global environment is also undergoing change. The intersections of change can create ambiguity and confusion, leading to paralysis for fear of making the wrong decision. As we discussed in Chapter 5 (*see also* pp. 95–115), resilience is the core component of evolving a robust approach to your career development and leadership. Building resilience helps to remove the fear associated with making 'bad' decisions. In this chapter, we expand on the idea of entrepreneurial leadership by helping you to move into the driving seat for your career. We present this through three key elements for your career: results-orientated, resourceful mindedness and relationship focus (Pasha, 2020).[44] In addition, we discuss the growing presence of activism in careers and through work. Activism

---

[44]Pasha, N. (2020) 'Responding to career uncertainty: Applying a dual-empathy approach to career development using corporate strategy theory'. *Journal of the National Institute for Career Education and Counselling*, 44(1), 44-50.

is increasingly a platform for purpose-based leadership, but to manage this well needs a careful and considered approach in your leadership development.

Pivoting careers is 'careering' for the next normal

With the range of choices available during your career, the idea of 'careering' can sound like a runaway horse or a go-kart hurtling off-course. As careers have evolved, modern theory has also evolved for individuals to recognize their power as agents of change. Jane Cathrall, Head of Talent Acquisition and Development for the Bank of England identifies the radical shift in thinking: 'Climbing the career ladder is a lot less straightforward than historically, there is no longer one, predictable route to follow and organizations and individuals are struggling to reconcile this. I observe both organizations and individuals still trapped in the mind-set of progression through promotion rather than skills building. This can result in early gains but longer term stagnation.'

With greater disparity of choice, people face more freedom in their career decisions. Freedom in itself does not come untethered, but recognizing what it brings is essential to success. When discussing the freedom around decisions regarding holiday time or expenses (and taking a radical approach to remove strict policy) at Netflix, Founder and CEO Reed Hastings explains the intrinsic link between freedom and responsibility – what he calls 'F&R'. This means providing greater freedom for decisions, which allows individuals greater independence, but this comes with the recognition of responsibility around the decisions. If you recognize that you have greater agency over your career, this is also aligned with greater individual responsibility around your career progression.

Building a successful career seems like a structured, well thought through approach. Often, when you read profiles and biographies of successful leaders their narrative sounds like a series of well-planned decisions, thought through and leading to career progression in a linear and consistently upward manner. In reality, successful career progression is a combination of art and science and involves learning from mistakes, learning from reading the environment and sense-making – and also undertaking actual learning and development. Building a successful career depends on deep expertise, a proven track record, along with the foresight to spot opportunities and networks to leverage for opportunities.

If you recognize your career is within a dynamic structure then you are better prepared for changes and able to pivot. Professor Yehuda Baruch, Professor of Management at the University of Southampton, UK, describes how workers are based in this ecosystem and need to be aware and respond to three distinct branches: interconnectedness, interactions and interdependencies.[45]

> **Interconnectedness** is the key characteristic of an ecosystem, manifested by interactions and enacted through interdependencies.

---

[45]Baruch & Rousseau (2018); Baruch et al. (2016).

Interactions take place, some more and some less significant than others, starting from the basic transactional exchange of labour for wages and at the firm level, expressed as the meeting of policies (local, national, transnational) with organizational strategies.

Interdependencies have of course been inbuilt into organizations ever since the Industrial Revolution, but in the post-modern environment they are characterized as VUCA (Volatile, Uncertain, Complex and Ambiguous).

The ecosystem approach helps to build an understanding of the interrelatedness between personal connections, relationships and the impact of change at individual and organizational levels. Of course, there is also the chance of encounters, opportunities emerging from new connections. Academics Robert Pryor and Jim Bright published research on the Chaos Theory of Careers (CTC) suggesting that while career outcomes are very much influenced by chance, you can harness skills and career management techniques to strengthen a positive mindset towards this uncertainty.[46] A CTC approach provides four specific pillars for career development:

- *Open-mindedness and curiosity for new opportunities:* Think now that a rigid career approach will limit career opportunities as chance events mean that they might not happen. Instead it is important that individuals take

---

[46]Pryor, R.G. & Bright, J.E. (2014) 'The Chaos Theory of Careers (CTC): Ten years on and only just begun'. *Australian Journal of Career Development*, 23(1), pp.4-12.

an approach that enables them to stay open-minded, explorative and curious to opportunities and adopt a proactive attitude;

- *Risk orientation:* A CTC approach suggests that by adopting an approach that encourages chance events, it is important to develop a positive approach to change, such as taking risks to try new opportunities, rather than staying with existing career ideas;

- *Understand the importance of self-reliance:* As career opportunities will arise at unexpected times, an individual has to be driven and motivated to keep going in difficulties, as well as having the ability to respond to a new opportunity when it does arrive;

- *Create supportive relationships:* Essential to adopting a CTC approach is ensuring that individuals can reflect on career opportunities as they arise and build effective networks in order to develop feedback opportunities.

We will come back to these areas later in this chapter and throughout the rest of the book. By now, you are starting to recognize your immense power in your ability to shape and control your career, especially amid great uncertainty, chaos and change. Daniel Susskind, author of *A World Without Work: Technology, Automation, and How We Should Respond*, explains the challenges in predicting career shifts but also emphasizes the need to think differently about reskilling in order to ensure we remain productive. He observes that despite the immense amount of time and attention invested in what the future of work might look like, speculating about the capabilities of machines in relations to humans, the reality is a world with far fewer opportunities for people to work. We think as long as we can repurpose our set of skills and talent, our human capital, then we can continue to find work. While this is true up to a point, the challenges we face are still ambiguous and we need to think radically differently about careers to become more adept at building necessary creativity and open-mindedness.

In the face of immense uncertainty and turbulence it can become all too easy to be pulled in directions you may not plan or even want to go in. If that sounds far-fetched, how many times have you spoken to someone who seems to have 'fallen' into a career, especially after graduation or key milestone events? Perhaps this is close to your own experience? To identify opportunities that are genuine leaps for you, having a clear sense of purpose is essential as a guide.

Recognizing your drivers

Throughout this book, we have emphasized the importance of entrepreneurial leaders recognizing the impact of emergent technologies; the same importance applies to every individual as you consider the impact and potential developments for your career. Can you visualize what your current job will look like in two, five or 10 years? A two-year time frame is relatively easy, even if the prospects are not positive. On the back of the disruption from COVID-19 coupled with the upheaval of emerging technology, it's harder to imagine the change over five years, and 10 may well seem like a lifetime away. Let's go slowly and create a way to understand and recognize incremental changes that will stack up to immense changes.

Remember the questions you considered at the beginning of this book: What drives you? What do you hope your career will allow you to achieve that can impact your world? It's all too easy to get caught up in grand visions and plans and there is no rule book, but in setting a purpose, it has to matter to you – this is your life. By focusing on your drivers, your purpose, you focus on the impact without being limited by a specific role. This approach allows you to identify different routes to achieve your goals and more importantly, adapt to the changes in the landscape and equally importantly, the ability to stretch your goals and aspirations.

While finding a purpose might sound grandiose to some of you, there are more pragmatic reasons why purpose is a strong driver for career success. Herminia Ibarra, Professor of Organisational Behaviour, at London Business School, explained the impact of leadership in a *Harvard Business Review* article: 'People become leaders by internalizing a leadership identity and developing a sense of purpose. Internalizing a sense of oneself as a leader is an iterative process. A person asserts leadership by taking purposeful action.'[47] When a sense of purpose creates goals aligned with personal values and work to advance the collective good, then individuals develop effective leadership attributes.

---

[47]https://hbr.org/2013/09/women-rising-the-unseen-barriers

A clearly defined purpose and goals with strong internal alignment enables leaders to create a vision and then take action to mobilize resources.

A strong sense of commitment to a greater good provides a compelling reason and often presents a plan that may seem beyond reasonable in a rational sense. Consider, for example, a project in Cairo, Egypt. A project of transformation: turning a 30-hectare site that had become a dumping ground for the city waste into a park. The seed of the idea began in 1984 when the Aga Khan, Head of the Aga Khan Development Network (AKDN), visited Cairo and spotted an opportunity to bring greenery into the city. Over the course of 21 years and following the removal of 1.5 million cubic metres of rubble and soil, in excess of US$ 30 million was invested in the park. This work unexpectedly led to the excavation and extensive restoration of the twelfth-century Ayyubid wall, as well as the renovation of housing in the local area, and investment in community infrastructure, including the building of a school, providing healthcare facilities and creating apprenticeship programmes and micro-credit facilities.[48]

In 2006, a year after the park was formally opened, it was included in the prestigious list of the 60 World's Greatest Places – Project for Public Spaces – a significant accolade for what was for decades the city dump. This project is certainly inspirational, combining an ambitious vision, broad purpose and strong values and commitment

---

[48]https://www.akdn.org/gallery/creating-urban-oasis-al-azhar-park-cairo-egypt

to seeing this goal through over an extraordinarily long time period. But what is extraordinary is that the approach to this project is consistent with the hundreds of initiatives under the AKDN, demonstrating that this holistic approach to vision, planning and implementation is a blueprint that runs across all the programmes. This example demonstrates ambitious leadership, as described by Ibarra: 'This allows them [leaders] to look beyond the status quo to what is possible ... Such leaders are seen as authentic and trustworthy because they are willing to take risks in the service of shared goals. By connecting others to a larger purpose, they inspire commitment, boost resolve, and help colleagues find deeper meaning in their work.'

Dynamic capabilities to career dynamism

Being able to lead and navigate your career during uncertainty and turbulence sounds logical enough, but in reality, how do you achieve this? In Chapter 5 we discussed Naeema's model of career dynamics (*see also*, pp. 106–105) and we will revisit this by using corporate strategy theory and dynamic capabilities developed by David Teece, Professor of Business Administration at Haas School of Business, University of California, Berkeley, to explain how organizations and individuals adapt during turbulence (2007). Dynamic capabilities are key strategic corporate competencies adopted by firms to establish competitive advantage. As we have discussed in earlier chapters in this book, some companies prospered despite the turbulence resulting from the global pandemic, but we also know a large number of companies failed. In considering performance through the lens of dynamic capabilities, we examine how organizations have inherent abilities to evolve rapidly and this momentum provides the basis for sustainable growth. At the heart of performance, success or failure lies human capital and how leadership teams identified changes, made decisions and implemented strategies. Investing in life-long employability has now become an imperative for every individual to maintain their relevance for work and even society and we will focus more attention on this in Chapter 9. Human capital can be folded into what is described by David Teece as 'Dynamic Microfoundations' (which include people skills) needed for the application of a dynamic capability for a firm and outlines the critical microfoundations people skills needed as:

- To be able to scan and analyze market changes and make interpretive choices based on the data;
- Adopting creative and innovative thinking to enable new products and services to meet changing customer needs;
- Developing strong relationships and social contacts to enable a better understanding of a market.

From this foundation, career dynamism emerged as a new approach to career development during turbulence and uncertainty. Central to this is the concept that to manage change and uncertainty, workers need adaptive and proactive career behaviours – and these same qualities are desirable for corporate success.

Getting personal with career dynamism

Firms rely on building competitive advantage for business growth by recruiting people with key skills and abilities in order to meet their strategic goals. Individual workers for personal ambition or economic interest will take up work. Therefore, as far as possible a career model should offer value to *both* workers and firms and create such a 'dual empathy' framework (skills that both the organization and employee benefit from) with these three key factors:

1) Key competencies;
2) Key personality traits;
3) Career resilience – which we saw in Chapter 5 (*see also* pp. 95–115)

The connections between these factors are illustrated in the figure below. This framework provides a three-part process for dynamic career management in the next normal. The framework is based on research carried out by Naeema, studying people who took uncertain non-linear career paths and were successful compared to those in successful linear careers.[49] As such, a new model of personal career development delivery is proposed based on these findings.

---

[49]Pasha, (2020), 44–50.

For those wanting to know the workings, this model was developed by researching people who took these two different paths and comparing the differences using multivariate analysis, correlations and discriminant analysis. The resulting career dynamism model incorporates the main findings from this study in relation to demands of employers and career self-management in a changing world of work. During the research process, when analyzing key factors in all the models there were key behaviours and traits that influenced career outcomes and these were combined to develop the career dynamism model. This model highlights key attributes for people to develop and starts with a capability to have a results focus mindset, then a capability to manage resources and situations well and finally, a capability to work with people effectively in order to achieve desired outcomes, as outlined below:

Part 1 – Results orientation: There will be a need for a proactive and results focus for an effective career self-management approach. To stay motivated and focused, it is necessary to 'put the effort in' and keep an eye on the end goal. Therefore, ability in *Achieving* will be needed to create an effective career strategy, given its alignment to career self-reliance and goal setting. *Conscientiousness* is needed in order to stay on goal and to keep renewing and adapting skills is key to success, which requires *Energy & Initiative* to stay motivated and to continue to maintain *Energy & Initiative*, as securing and maintaining a job takes effort and working in continuous change requires energy and tenacity. *Initiative* is critical in reviewing new options and working in uncertainty and managing challenges as they arise.

Part 2 – Resourceful mindedness: There will be a need to be resourceful and use one's own skills to work out ideas and solutions, both in work and in career strategy in a new working environment, especially as 'work' may not be linear and traditional, while career 'ownership' is more likely to be located with the worker. Therefore, there will be a need to demonstrate career resilience to manage change, chaos and uncertainty well and in particular, to show personal *Self-reliance*, as this demonstrates autonomy and resourcefulness in problem solving and an ability to deal with difficulties.

Resilience shows a self-minded approach to a career and aligns with aspects of *Self-determined Behaviours*. There is a need to demonstrate *Openness to Experiences* to be able to meet and create new opportunities, showing curiosity, openness to risk, diversity in its broadest sense and tolerance to 'the new', which may well be new forms of employment. An openness to experiences trait also shows adaptability, which will be key. There is a need to show *Analysis* as continuously evaluating new opportunities and challenges will be the norm in the new world of work, static careers and jobs being less common. It is therefore important to apply critical thinking and analyze new situations, opportunities and career options with an effective analytical problem-solving mindset. This aligns with dynamic capabilities not just to enable a firm's strategic goals to be met, but also to encourage a worker to continually be reviewing and evolving personal career goals.

Career dynamism: a nine-factor career dynamism model for the new world of work

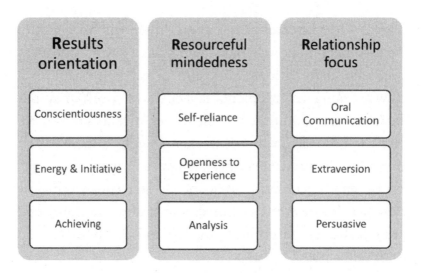

Part 3 – Relationship focus: Relationship building is paramount to success in a changing world of work and can be demonstrated by showing skills in *Oral Communication*. There will be an increased need to continuously build new and effective networks as new networks will form and reform in a more dynamic and fluid working world. With complex new forms of employment (e.g. gig/contingent), it will be essential to be able to hold conversations with new people in order to build productive new relationships. These conversations should afford the ability to connect with people and build effective, strong networks and this is enabled by showing *Extraversion* behaviours of talking, connecting and engaging.

By the way, if you are an introvert, don't think you're done for. This extroversion is from the Jungian psychology definition of where people find energy (https://www.britannica.com/science/introvert). It is not about how people come across and it's not a measure of shyness and dancing on tables-ness. All it means is that chatting and building relationships are things you need to do and these often are easier for extroverts. Maybe you already do this, but if not, think about how to stretch yourself a bit here. If you are extroverted, this might still feel uncomfortable, but as we saw in chaos careers (*see also* pp. 158–159), networking can reap good results and it all starts with being able to talk well, listen well and lead with empathy. This approach can be viewed as 'adopted behaviours' needed for successful career development.

There will be a need for workers to be able to understand their own skills and strengths, have confidence (self-efficacy) in themselves, and show competency in negotiating new forms of work and career by showing *Persuasiveness*. This skill will also be a key requirement for workers to negotiate their way in a more dynamic working environment, as well as working across differing work/company structures.

So, look at all the nine factors here and ask yourself the following questions:

- How comfortable are you with each box; where were you a year ago?
- What has changed for you compared to 12 months ago?
- Where are your strengths?
- Where do you need to pay attention for more development?
- What measurable goals do you want set for the next six, 12 and 18 months?

Deconstructing the big pieces in career development allows you to deconstruct the key elements and helps you to get practical and focus on specific areas. By demystifying this area, you can tackle each area in manageable, bite-sized pieces and pay attention to what matters to you right now and in the near future for your career. At this point we will return your attention to the discussion in Chapter 5 on resilience (*see also* pp. 95–115): self-resilience is critical to this framework. An important aspect of managing uncertainty found in this study is building self-reliance. Naeema found the most significant factor within career resilience is self-reliance, demonstrated through people taking control and ownership of their career journeys, i.e. being responsible for their own learning and development, taking on more responsibility and being independent. Our research found self-reliant people can survive better in a working world that has more contingent work, occupational hybridization, side hustling, gig working and greater uncertainty with fewer stable jobs. The data shows that the dynamic-type career people had higher levels of self-reliance than traditional-type career people.[50]

The growing focus on career drivers is leading to an increase in social change and activism in the workplace. Activism in the workplace is a new and emerging area of attention and received a significant boost in 2020 as a result of climate change, Black Lives Matter protests and heightened inequalities emerging from the global pandemic.

---

[50]Pasha (2019).

What part does corporate activism
play in your career?

There was a time when workplace culture and values shaped every element of your working identity with very little flexibility. Over time, however, progressive organizations have adapted and flexed to create space to incorporate and even encourage individuals to introduce social change. Of course, this doesn't mean the situation presents a free-for-all for activism, but with greater openness, it does become easier to share their views and find ways to activate their thinking. It can be easy to get caught up in the energy and opportunity around social activism, but once you pick up the placard for what you want to do, then you become visible in your association in relation to the cause.

We understand there's a real dilemma around people coming into the workplace and wanting to take on an activist approach to introduce social justice. In many places, work is rapidly becoming a catalyst for change. At an individual level, the confidence and desire for activism will change over your career. If you begin with a strong sense of justice this may get challenged as your status increases with career progression. And yet, as you get promotions you achieve increased social status or start to be taken more seriously as a leader, but there's a degree of having to conform in order to become that leader as well. When you look at your organizations, even the most senior and distinguished leaders were passionate about elements of social change earlier in their lives and careers. Examples of such leaders are Rose Marcario, recent President and CEO of Patagonia, who under her reign quadrupled sales of their outdoor clothing and equipment, while at same time contributing more to environmental groups than at any time previously. We will share more examples throughout this chapter.

We can see things are changing – numerous conversations and workshops in 2020 demonstrated the emphasis of senior leaders on providing space and building skills to enable conversations with a strong social emphasis. Much of this momentum emerges from the diversity and inclusion agenda and starts with conversations around difference, equality and inclusion. Over time, we know that these areas rapidly gather pace and the momentum moves into other areas, bringing about change to the culture and goals in organizations.

The year 2020 was the year when employee activism was recognized as a defining area in the workplace.[51] We believe you can wear your activist T-shirt in the office – if it meets the values of the organization. Most organizations now have a stronger alignment on discrimination and climate. If you speak against your organization, there may be difficulties ahead and you will need to think about the balance of wanting to bring about change in relation to the pushback to maintain the status quo.

And how do you do this? By you deciding on what is important to you, since most organizations are fairly risk-averse. However, unless organizations also take more of a stand, they risk being known for having weak corporate

---

[51]https://www.hrzone.com/lead/culture/the-rise-of-employee-activism-a-defining-issue-for-hr-in-2020

social responsibility (CSR) policies as they do a disservice to everyone. It's becoming more part of the corporate landscape and the responsibility of companies to make the world better. Andy Noronha, Director of People, Strategy and Transformation at Cisco explains the opportunity: 'New digital technologies and processes, fueled by creativity and innovation, are reshaping industries and societies. They have the potential to accelerate social change by connecting individuals and communities to information and resources, providing access to new economic opportunities, and enabling equal access to public and social services.'

We see that in terms of talent attraction and acquisition; people want to be associated with the companies where there's an alignment of values or sense of purpose. At one time, taking a knee was not acceptable but as the Black Lives Matter movement gained exposure, we saw and continue to see it accepted. Even corporate culture is moving towards actively rather than passively making a stand against discrimination.

In response to the protests around Black Lives Matter and the death of George Floyd, companies opened conversations about race and inequality, but also went further by investing in communities to start to address these divides. PepsiCo, Inc. committed to programmes over five years with more than US$400 million in investment to address black inequality, including US $25 million for a scholarship programme for college and US $50 million to support black-owned small enterprises.[52] Perhaps the most innovative and interesting

---

[52]https://www.forbes.com/sites/shaheenajanjuhajivrajeurope/2020/10/31/performance-with-purpose-pepsico-getting-beyond-words/?sh=19e98205d803

part of this initiative was the commitment to an art exhibition titled 'Black Art Rising', creating a time capsule to record the BLM protests and providing a catalyst for important conversations around systemic racism and racial injustice.

In the summer of 2020, Selfridges, the oldest department store in London, took a radical step in bringing activism to the heart of business with Project Earth, an initiative focusing on climate change and retail. The various initiatives under this umbrella include a concession stand for Oxfam International to trade second-hand clothes, opportunities to purchase vintage high-end luxury products and a department where domestic electrical items could be repaired.

On the surface, this might not seem revolutionary, but the context of a high-end luxury department store transforming its supply chain along climate goals is setting a high bar for the retail sector. Selfridges has shared a commitment to science-based targets and achieving net zero carbon by 2050, in line with the Paris Agreement (an international treaty on climate change that participating nation states will be bound by). Alannah Weston, Chair for Selfridges Group Foundation, explained how Project Earth was a decade-long commitment to climate change: 'Selfridges has been focused on changing mindsets around sustainability, both inside our industry and in conversation with our customers. Out of the global pandemic has come an understanding of how fragile and complex our systems are and how our planet and people can benefit if we act collectively with a shared purpose. More than ever, we must double down on our efforts to reinvent retail with sustainability at its heart and a way of working that is regenerative for humans and nature. Achieving our ambitions won't be easy, but we are in a unique position to work with our team members, partners and customers to co-create change and explore possibilities for a sustainable future.'[53]

What is even more interesting about the Selfridges model is how the company has encouraged activism among its staff to influence social change initiatives across the organization. In the same article, Daniella Vega, then Director of Sustainability at Selfridges, describes how the organization adopted this approach in 2011 for another environmental initiative, Project Ocean, an interesting project that connects retail and climate, resulting in a long-term partnership with the Zoological Society of London to protect oceans from overfishing and plastic pollution. She describes this approach as 'retail activism', where a strong retail brand can leverage its influence to catalyze change: 'We brought together the power of the platform that we have and because we are an aggregator of brands and partnership, we used that power to bring together different players around environmental issues. We brought together NGOs such as Greenpeace, the Zoological Society of London and politicians, policy-makers and customers, brands and team members. We were able to amplify the conversation and shine a light on it and use our forum as a retailer to take steps to do better as a business. One outcome was a commitment never to sell or serve endangered fish and we used our stores as campaigns.

---

[53]Janjuha-Jivraj, S. (2020) https://www.forbes.com/sites/shaheenajanjuhajivrajeurope/2020/09/02/how-selfridges-is-building-on-diverse-talent-to-make-create-a-new-sustainable-business-as-usual-model/?sh=7b30989761bf

Using our windows and our store to help educate, inspire and offer proactive ways to customers to make a change in their everyday lives.'

There are many more examples that share similar experiences of change and impact, but we also offer a word of caution. The landscape is still nuanced and you need to think carefully about which battles you choose. What we are saying is that being you, bringing your values in on Monday to work, will be part of the new normal. It will be a little rocky at times, so tread carefully, but another super-hero skill is really knowing what you stand for.

Recognize that who you are matters and a) don't hide yourself away, and b) stand up for what you believe. At the same time, there is a need to consider how you land your messages and how you engage with colleagues. Within the workplace, you are still working in a culture and where you have strong views in an area you will need to be mindful of how these land with others. Developing your negotiation skills and sensitivities about how your views land with colleagues and even senior leaders is important, so it's always useful to ask a trusted colleague to sense-check your thinking.

So, taking action on key issues does come at a price. And we're talking about activism in all the ways you work – gig, flexible, remote working, full-time, part-time, permanent. Whatever its form, you might think about at what point your work becomes part of your activism or your activism becomes part of your work, or do you keep that side of you quiet and do your protests at the weekend? In a sense, this is about your values and identity.

How activist is the future of work?

Younger generations are entering a world where volatility and non-linearity in careers will increase, with greater levels of occupational hybridization and contingent/gig working. Our research looked at Gen Z in the workplace. The psychological contract of work is changing: with our employers no longer offering lifetime employment, they can still expect workers to be so loyal that, they are defined by the organization they work for. Gen Zs show they do value the company brand and show loyalty – but not blind loyalty; I'm not sure as many of the newer generations still want to say 'I'm an IBM-er' (or wherever they work). And according to research from Henley Business School called Four Better or Four Worse, which looks at a four-day week and generational differences in the workplace, nearly half (47 per cent) of employees want a career that helps them make a positive impact on society, but two-thirds (66 per cent) of Gen Z say this is the case. They do still need effective work structures that offer some security but also work that is good for flexibility and skills building. So, say we went to a four-day week, Gen Zs might prefer more flexible working, allowing for free time for non-work. They also seek companies that care for employee wellbeing and the climate too – ones that are very values driven.

For Gen Zs and Millennials entering the workforce, then, we see that while pay and career progression is still important to them, sharper awareness of social, political and environmental causes is increasing. More than ever, younger generations want their values reflected in their employer's values and many will use this as a deciding factor when selecting a future employer. The package is no longer enough for the new generation of employees; the company's position on key social issues will also determine which ones are viewed as desirable places to work.

The lines between drivers and work become powerful tools to develop your career and build career dynamism that is essential to maintain agency over your career. At the same time, these elements are increasingly influencing the workplace and create opportunities for more open conversations around social change and connection between business, government and civil society. Many of the skills that emerge from engaging in social change are critical to career development and we will discuss these in greater detail in Chapter 11. At the moment, for many organizations, social change is similar to that experience of dipping a toe in the water: it will be a shock and deeply uncomfortable – some will retract and return to beach, others will acclimatize and go in a bit deeper and become comfortable with this approach in their business as usual. Of course, it goes without saying that companies that demonstrate a stronger culture of dynamism are more likely to be more open and robust in handling activism – and these are interesting organizations we want to follow.

CHAPTER NINE

Learning Smarter

If we recognize the value of life-long learning, why is it so hard to shift our thinking towards education? In essence, we are socialized from a very young age to consider education in blocks and something we do in preparation to work, and maybe something to return to when we want to change direction. In terms of education, one message we have constantly reinforced in this book is the importance of continuous learning. However it is described – reskilling, upskilling, lifelong learning, even life-wide learning – the bottom line is you need to access new skills to remain relevant. Skills are your new currency and without continuous investment, you risk becoming irrelevant.

Reskilling and upskilling generates a range of areas that need more attention to provide specific areas of support and to ensure individuals access high-quality training that will provide access to new career opportunities. The digital skills shortage is a global crisis: a World Economic Forum report on digital inclusion indicates that 47 per cent of the world's population is unconnected and in lower-income countries only 32 per cent of the population has sufficient skills to complete basic tasks such as sending emails.[54] Across Europe, the figures are not much better, with the European Commission identifying that approximately 37 per cent of workers do not have the basic digital skills. Research by the Open University found that 88 per cent of organizations in the UK report a shortage in this area, severely damaging the capabilities of organizations to adopt and progress with digital technologies.[55] A report by Microsoft on the digital skills gap in the UK reinforces these worries: nearly two-thirds of employees in their data set agreed that they do not have the appropriate digital skills to fulfil new and emerging roles in their industry.[56]

This approach to education requires lateral thinking to keep engaging with learning, but we also need to get smarter and more nuanced about the type of education we are accessing. The challenge is for you to reframe your thinking to understand the immense power and opportunity of unlocking resources, for yourself and your work. Knowledge economies, the thrust of the fourth industrial revolution, can only prosper if the human, intellectual capital is continuously updated.

One of the greatest challenges with formal education is the infrastructure on which it is built; in Chapter 1, we discussed the impact of the Industrial Revolution on economic growth and social change and the proliferation of skills in workers (*see also* pp. 22–25). Basic literacy and numeracy skills needed to be taught efficiently and these

[54]https://www.weforum.org/reports/accelerating-digital-inclusion-in-the-new-normal
[55]http://www.open.ac.uk/business/bridging-the-digital-divide
[56]https://www.microsoft.com/en-gb/home/digital-skills/unlocking-potential/

demands created the foundation of formal education, which ultimately spread across the world. The late Sir Ken Robinson, one of the greatest advocates for reforming education, explained in his powerful Ted Talk, 'Do Schools Kill Creativity?', the need for efficiency driving education systems and ultimately creating barriers for powerful learning. In one of his final statements before his untimely demise after a short battle with cancer in 2020, he identified the paradox we face: 'It is often said that education and training are the keys to the future. They are, but a key can be turned in two directions. Turn it one way and you lock resources away, even from those they belong to. Turn it the other way and you release resources and give people back to themselves.'

Let's dive in and understand what we can do to turn the key the right way and unlock opportunities for us. Motivation is probably far more prevalent than we realize; the statistics we shared at the beginning of this chapter demonstrate a recognition of the problem with the skills gap. In the Digital Skills report by Microsoft, Carol Stubbings, Global Tax and Legal Services Leader for the PwC Network[57], points out: 'Companies that have invested in upskilling have seen better employee satisfaction. Because do not forget, people want to be reskilled. They know they need to learn new things to be relevant.' Inevitably, when resources are tight, particularly during recessions, and ironically at a time when reskilling is most needed, investment in

---

[57]https://www.pwc.com/gx/en/services/people-organisation/upskill-my-workforce-for-the-digital-world.html

this area dries up. More than a third of leaders in the UK identify the lack of financial resources for skilling up for the next stage of work developments, followed by 28 per cent not having a digital skills investment strategy and 23 per cent not knowing which initiatives to focus on. Having read this book, most leaders will have addressed the latter two barriers and no doubt identified resources for necessary skilling.

Learning how we learn

The pandemic and disruption to formal education has catalyzed the long-overdue need to transform what and how we absorb education. In this book, we have spent a great deal of time discussing how we navigate and work with more sophisticated developments in emerging technologies. We also need to think about how we invest time and effort in our own software – our brain. From the moment we are born, our brains are learning; we are absorbing and taking in new information from our surroundings and we learn to process that data into usable information. In our formative years, from birth to childhood and even into our teens, our curriculum is predetermined by parents, carers, family and then schools and teachers. Our software is a reflection of our environment, leading to what world-renowned author on future technologies, Max Teggart, calls 'Life 2.0'. Our hardware is our DNA, which stores approximately 1 gigabyte (as a guide, this is equivalent to sending or receiving approximately 1,000 emails). In contrast, our software stores all our memories and skills, occupying around 1,000 terabytes of information. Learning is essential to our survival. Our synapses grow 100,000 times from birth and need constant input to keep growing and connecting; our brains continue to learn by absorbing new stimuli and creating new synapses. Growing our software is automatic, but we have control over what and how we learn.

As we develop our competencies, a key element is to recognize our preferred styles of learning. Effective learning combines the four areas: conceptualizing abstract thinking, observations, experimentation and experience. Without getting too detailed about the different styles of learning, we can categorize learning into two main areas: theoretical and experiential (or contextual learning). David Kolb, the eminent educational theorist based at Case Western Reserve University in Ohio, devised a simple but very effective framework to demonstrate the main ways in which we learn and that having experiences can enable us to learn more effectively and this new learning is something we can reapply.

Each of these areas is important in learning. For leadership, development experiential learning is particularly key and the most challenging to access (more on how to navigate this in Chapter 10). The more comfortable you are in recognizing how you learn most effectively, the more you can access knowledge in a style that suits you. Today, more than ever, the channels for education are wider and more creative, and through new frontiers in technology, more accessible than ever before. Learning in the workplace will need to be redressed, particularly as hybrid working becomes normalized. Some of the traditional approaches to learning will need to adapt quickly.

Timo Hannay, founder of SchoolDash and a non-executive director of SAGE Publishing and Arden University, summarizes the environment; 'There's been a huge fragmentation of education channels that's somewhat akin to the fragmentation of media that we saw during the first 25 years of the web (like media, it will surely start to consolidate again as the winners acquire or outcompete the also-rans.) The strongest established players won't go away, but they will adapt (witness HarvardX). Meanwhile, hundreds of other players – from The Teaching Company and Code with Google to Khan Academy and Mathologer – are providing new ways to learn. For anyone with insatiable curiosity, this is surely the best time in human history to be alive. The challenge is to be able to find and select the most appropriate services from the myriad options on offer.'

Leaders are not born…

Before we proceed any further, let's burst an important myth: leadership is neither a trait nor a behaviour that you are born with. There is research to suggest a specific genotype in humans is correlated with the likelihood of holding leadership positions[58] but, this study concludes that

---

[58]De Neve, J., Mikhaylov, S., Dawes, C., Christakis, N. & Fowler, J. (2021) 'Born to lead? A twin design and genetic association study of leadership role occupancy'. *Leadership Quarterly*, 24(1); 45–60

even with the disposition of this gene towards leadership, environmental factors are a major influencer. Leadership can be learned – it is taught by providing frameworks, models and theories for students to understand. The other, and equally important side, of learning is in the application and evaluation of what works and where limitations exist. Leadership is often described as an art, but in reality, it is the accumulation of knowledge – learned theories, along with extensive experiences of doing and observing.

Embarking on an upskilling journey is complex, partly because the end goal is still unclear and also the motivations for learning as an adult need more attention for you to better understand what is driving you forwards. Motivation for learning is not a simple cause-and-effect relationship: in essence, it's complicated. We are driven by a combination of extrinsic and intrinsic factors. Extrinsic factors are externally driven, aligned with better career opportunities that lead to better financial incentives, the expectations of rewards beyond financial remuneration and explicit recognition for making an impact on changing the landscape. Intrinsic factors by contrast are internally driven: why you choose to take on new learning will be deeply embedded in how you see yourself and what drives you to keep learning. In the first instance, your reactions to changes in the workplace will help you identify your readiness to learn and upskill. Coping with current and anticipated changes will either leave you wanting to ignore everything or tackle the changes head-on. How you react will condition your intrinsic motivation and your willingness to continue learning.

Recognizing the value of ongoing learning as an essential component helps you gear up for career dynamism and also underpins the dynamism in the workplace. It's important to ask yourself these questions: What's going in your workplace? How is learning valued as the core of your work identity? The value of global companies relies extensively on the intellectual capital of their workforce; retaining talent is one issue. Ensuring employees are embarking on a journey of continuous learning and upskilling is essential to the survival and performance of the organization. Normalizing learning and upskilling is a core element of any profession requiring accredited members to embark on further skills development: whether you are a chartered accountant, marketer, lawyer or educator, compulsory continuing professional development (CPD) hours are mandated to validate your membership. What is more interesting is how organizations normalize learning in the culture of working, creating an expectation that colleagues will engage in reskilling annually in order to build their skills and update their knowledge and thinking. For example, IBM sets the expectation for colleagues to engage in 40 hours of training every year. Taking a curated learning approach, IBM employees have a choice about where they invest their learning, but creating a culture of ongoing learning is a primary driver in self-directed learning.

An uncomfortable but necessary truth is that we have to find ways to learn and re-educate ourselves in order to stay ahead of new technology. Daniel Susskind describes how we need to approach learning: 'Embracing life-long learning is a way of insuring ourselves against the unknowable demands that the working world of the future might make on us.' If we recognize that new technologies can be viewed as competition, where jobs will change and our status quo will be challenged, in order to maintain our relevance and longevity then we need to consider how we continue to renew – a mindset described by prolific leadership researcher and author Jim Collins, who said that we need to consider that 'we are never going to retire, but instead we will renew'.[59] Renewal creates a different mindset when we consider the need to update our wiring on a regular and continuous basis. As we recognize that these challenges create impetus for change, then we recognize that we need to get smarter about how we invest time and effort into learning.

How do you decide where to pay attention? This is where the skills we have discussed throughout this book become important in your decision making. How are you identifying trends in the roles and careers that interest you? In the absence of hard, specific facts to provide a clear route forwards, here are some questions for you to answer: Where are you gathering intelligence from? Whose perspectives influence your thinking? How are you building your network to stimulate new approaches to assessing this area? Timo Hannay identifies the shift in boundaries around education: 'The traditional education systems don't just teach, they also confer credentials. To complement traditional macro-credentials (like degrees) from established players (like

---

[59]https://howtoacademy.com/events/jim-collins-beyond-entrepreneurship/

universities), we're seeing a rise in micro-credentials (such as course certification) from non-traditional providers (starting with technology companies, but surely not limited to them). In the future, you may have a blue-chip company on your CV not because you worked there, but because they certified some of your training. Thus the boundary between educator and employer will get fuzzier.'

Beyond formal qualifications, it can be daunting to navigate how skills need attention – after all, learning is an investment of time, energy, money and hopes. The OECD collects data from over 40 countries/economies, generating an audit of key cognitive and workplace skills required for 'Individuals to participate in society and for economies to prosper'.[60] When you review the measures, they incorporate the basic skills but what is more illuminating is the inclusion of new skills – see the figure below. The new additions focus on the skills we have emphasized throughout this book to navigate the next normal. Look at the middle block – socio-emotional skills encompassing behaviours, beliefs, but also how connections and relationships are made with colleagues. Adaptive problem solving is particularly important in this discussion as it describes the ability of an individual to apply technology in solving problems and accomplishing complicated tasks. More explicitly, this metric measures whether an individual can solve multiple problems in parallel and identify opportunities for solving different issues that arise. As you read through this description, you start to get an idea of the higher level of skills, thinking and application

---

[60]https://www.oecd.org/skills/piaac/

that are important to determine your preparedness for navigating your leadership.

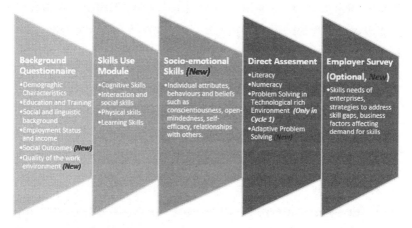

Source: OCED PIAAC[61]

When we consider these higher-level skills, we can consider them as meta-skills. Meta-skilling is identified as overriding skills that amplify and catalyze other skills (largely technical). Naeema's work on skilling for career progression clusters three areas that overarch everything we have discussed in this book and builds on the importance of meta-skilling.[62] Implementing meta-skills is similar to engaging high-order skills to allow you to implement your functional expertise with greater effectiveness. The specific nature of meta-skills varies according to the situation. However, Naeema argues that in response to new frontiers in technology, the three areas of focus are: human skills, agency and of course, technology. In Chapter 4 we discussed the key elements of

[61]https://www.oecd.org/skills/piaac/piaacdesign/
[62]Pasha (2020).

entrepreneurial leadership and the need to become very comfortable with data, technology and leadership (*see also* pp. 69–94). In this discussion on meta-skilling, some of the areas overlap directly with the earlier discussion – for example, technology (no surprises there) – while others complement entrepreneurial leadership – activism and human skills.

We have spent time addressing these individual areas: technology in Chapters 3 and 7, activism in Chapter 8 and leadership in Chapter 4. At this point, it's worth honing in specifically on human skills and why these matter not only for your career progression, but also for leadership development. Leadership guru Peter Drucker forecast the shift in focus in the workplace by asking the question in 2016: 'How can we make society both more productive and more humane?' At the time, the juxtaposition of these two elements may have raised eyebrows due to their contradictory nature. In Chapter 2, we discussed the impact of the pandemic unearthing and exacerbating inequalities in the workplace and across society. As this unfolded in 2020 and beyond, a great deal of attention focused on how to create more humane connections at work.

What does it mean to be human at work? How can you encourage and create conditions to strengthen human connections among your team and the organization? Meta skills for human connections emphasize empathy, creating meaningful connections with your colleagues to build trust and openness. Creating a strong foundation of trust starts with human connections, genuine interest in your colleagues – that goes far beyond the initial ice-breaker with your team. What really matters to them, what are their drivers, what are their work aspirations? If you are leading a team, no matter how big or small, what tone are you setting for your colleagues? How do you proactively encourage colleagues to share their views and more importantly, challenge assumptions? In Chapter 6, we discussed the impact of biases and groupthink (*see also* pp. 117–138). If you want your team to become more comfortable with creative thinking and risk-taking, then creating safety to share wacky ideas, question assumptions and challenge how things are done will only happen if you have invested considerable care and effort in building a culture of trust. As a leader, authenticity is essential – if you are genuinely interested and respect your team this is evident, not just during team bonding sessions, but especially during stressful times and when teams are stretched. Entrepreneurial leadership works at its best with pluralistic teams, where the individual differences and experiences of team members are celebrated and actively brought into conversations.

Collaboration is a natural partner for innovation and effective problem-solving, but again, the conditions need to be in place for this to work well. At its best, collaboration is a shared commitment to finding solutions, pooling the best resources, thinking and expertise. If you don't get this right, then you aren't collaborating but instead co-operating, which has its strengths. Co-operation works if you want two teams to work together while retaining themselves as individual entities, but if you want the exchange of ideas to shape and inform the thinking of both teams, then you need to be willing to invest in collaboration. This means upfront investment to allow colleagues to spend time building relationships of openness and trust, feeling comfortable in pushing back against ideas or calling out different ways to do things without causing offence. All of these elements are sensible but in practice can be incredibly difficult to achieve if you are caught up working with colleagues who are sensitive or don't have sufficient trust in each other.

We talked about Netflix's 4As to handle honest feedback effective in Chapter 4 and it's worth taking a moment to consider what happened the last time you received feedback: how did you respond, during and afterwards? Consider also the last time you gave feedback: how did you prepare and what impact did it have afterwards? Handling feedback is not easy as hardly anyone welcomes the perspective of being told what they are not doing well. Remember in Chapter 5, we talked about the brain and our emotions (*see also* pp. 100–103)? It's unsurprising that our reactions are more likely to be negative so we need to consciously find creative ways to elicit different reactions. Feedforward presents a different way to approach sensitive conversations of this nature in recognizing and valuing someone's work and providing constructive advice on what can be done even better next time.[63] Taking a feedforward approach allows individuals to hear positive views and remain open to feedback rather than shutting down into a defensive mode when they are being criticized.

---

[63]Janjuha-Jivraj, S. & Chisholm, K. (2015) *Championing Women Leaders Beyond Sponsorship*, Basingstoke: Palgrave MacMillan

How you react to this discussion on building relationships with colleagues will depend on your own experiences and how you view your working life. Wherever you land on this discussion, the future is clear: investing resources in what the OECD call 'socio-emotional skills' creates a strong basis to improve your meta-skills. At the same time as you recognize that learning is essential for your career dynamism and leadership progression, your journey will become more exciting and fulfilling. Not only will you be able to spot opportunities, but you'll also have the confidence and resources to take these opportunities and move into higher levels of leadership. The big takeaway from this chapter is that you need to develop agency for your learning – no one will take the responsibility for determining your career and what further skills you need to develop and leaders are already promoting this approach, as demonstrated by Jeff Phipps of ADP: 'Where people take ownership for their learning journey, that's where we see a real change of attitude. So I think in the same way as, you know, to me, it's right there with health right now, you can go, you know, if you're really committed to it, you say this is a lifestyle thing. This is not a diet, it's a lifestyle change, right? I'm not just going to have a portion of training and then go back to doing what I was doing before. I'm going to recognize that for me to be relevant and good, I think those two go together. I've got to commit to a journey of learning and I need to determine what that means for me because I'm two reasons: one is I'm probably more motivated than anyone else to look after myself, and secondly, I should have a better understanding of me than anyone else so when you put those two together...'

CHAPTER TEN

Ninja thinking for your career

'The harder I work, the luckier I get' – or do I?

As we've already discussed, career planning is a result of both internal and external influences. We know from the earlier chapters on chaos and dynamic careers (*see also* pp. 158–160 and 163–169) that successful career development to leadership means we work a tension between mastery and skill and fate or good fortune. We contend with our own experiences, which create our values and ideals about what makes a 'good career' and 'good leadership', which is influenced by society, family, education and experiences – and our personalities. We talked about self-efficacy and career resilience built through different experiences. This means when we talk about successful leaders, there is often a tension between mastery and skill and fate or good fortune. The quote above is often used by Shaheena when challenging senior leaders (more often than not women), who attribute their success to luck[64] – either, 'I was lucky to have a good boss' or 'I was fortunate to be in a position...' While there may be an element of truth in this, ascribing

---

[64]This quote has its origins attributed to a selection of individuals, including Frank Sinatra, Samuel Goldwyn and even Thomas Jefferson. In any case, the sentiment matters more than the source.

success to luck removes the agency of the individual and their work and effort in their achievements.

Whatever your views on fate, the reality is complex. Opportunities will present themselves in abundance but unless you understand how to develop the skills and the ability to demonstrate your capabilities, it will be harder to realize the career progression you want. The key to success is achieving a balance between grabbing opportunities while building skills and developing important resources to navigate your career. In this chapter, we will share our ninja resources: what makes the difference to super-boost your career. One of the challenges when discussing career progression is the recognition that not everyone has the same starting point and there is often a misplaced view that if everyone is treated equally, they have a fair shot at achieving leadership roles. While equality is admirable and endearing, it can also cause challenges in assumptions. An alternative and more effective approach is to consider an equitable approach in understanding career progression.

We spend time in this chapter focusing on the necessary resources for marginalized groups and specifically, women in leadership. If you don't fall into the categories targeted into the diversity agenda, we encourage you to read through these areas anyway to prepare yourself to become a leader who encourages a pluralistic culture.

Adopting an equitable approach requires a leadership approach that is far more nuanced than the traditional sledgehammer approach that has dominated the business world for decades. Although more effort is required with this approach, it fits well with the increasing recognition that we don't have a one-size-fits-all model of leadership. The hundreds of leadership models demonstrate the variety of how different styles and characteristics underpinning leadership behaviours in different cultures. Strong and diverse teams of leaders require a robust pipeline of talent and over the last decade a great deal of attention has focused on the barriers that impact the career progression among individuals who are from minority backgrounds.

Gender leadership, women holding board and executive leadership positions, has been an area of great focus since 2010 mobilized by the Davies review of Women on Boards in the United Kingdom, and similar attention being paid in the US and many European countries.[65] Over the last decade, most countries have started to address the barriers impacting career progression for women; international networks provide the basis for benchmarking progress. The W20 was launched in 2016 as an official G20 engagement group promoting women's economic empowerment as an integral part of the G20 process.[66] Discussions focus on pay, technology and childcare provisions as key areas of focus for gender progression into leadership, while the 2018 Commonwealth Heads of Government meeting addressed the disparity around women in leadership across all areas.[67] The World Economic Forum produces an annual index on gender equality and female participation in the labour

---

[65]https://www.gov.uk/government/news/women-on-boards
[66]http://sdg.iisd.org/events/g20-women-20-w20-summit-2021/
[67]https://www.yonetimkurulundakadin.org/assets/node_modules/source/pdf/commonwealth_report_4.pdf

market.[68] The consistent attention to gender leadership is essential as the expected ripple effect of progress does not occur. Former CEO of Lloyd's of London and Portfolio Director, Dame Inga Beale describes the challenges still facing organizations tackling gender diversity: 'I believe that many organizations have started late. Building a robust pipeline can take years. First of all you have to get the talent in the front door so you've got to really work on attracting talent. Secondly you've got to be able to retain that talent. In my experience many women choose to leave the world of work or their particular employer because the culture itself is not inclusive. Having to play politics or having to put up with microaggressions means that many women will say "life is too short, why should I put up with this? I'm going off to do my own thing" and they will choose to leave the corporate world.' The key message here is that the barriers that impact career progression for women take a lot longer to dismantle and even when organizations undergo the experience of exogenous shocks that will impact the culture of the institution. Change does not automatically create more opportunities for women.

If we turn our attention to other areas of protected characteristics, the results are even more disturbing. Diversity through the race or ethnicity lens is steeped in cultural sensitivities and political correctness, not to mention legislation in some countries (including the US) that make it almost impossible to monitor and track the real picture for career progression. The current debate around

---

[68]https://www.weforum.org/reports/gender-gap-2020-report-100-years-pay-equality

race gets stuck at the first hurdle of language with emotional reactions to the appropriateness of current labels around: people/person of colour (an American term), BAME – Black, Asian, Minority Ethnic, used in the UK. There is even more confusion in determining whether a person is classified by their race, nationality, ethnic origin, cultural background or religion. Humans are a messy combination of different elements and using one label often causes resentment and does more harm than good. The conversations around how organizations address ethnicity in the workplace still need to pay greater attention to addressing the barriers that lead to the current gaps in leadership based on ethnicity. When we consider wider areas such as sexual orientation, disability and social class, the area becomes a thick soup of confusion full of good intentions, but with so many differences to push forwards on that the reality can become confusing.

Marginalized groups in organizations find their career progression is stunted by lack of access to networks and relationships with senior leaders. The data shows that despite the wide range of initiatives targeting women's careers since 2010, progress has been sporadic and hugely dependent on the enthusiasm and commitment of key individuals. Attention has focused on different stages of the pipeline – from early levels to executive and board leadership – but with all the different levers, it's difficult to maintain consistent attention. Any organization that is serious about diversity needs resources to provide clarity of thought and build a roadmap aligned to the strategic direction of the organization.

Although the Diversity and Inclusion (D&I) lead is not solely responsible for the D&I success in the organization, their efforts are hugely hampered without adequate resources for leadership support, people and budgets. Diversity is a proactive approach to culture change in an organization but it can't be something that is done to a group of people who are struggling to get into the leadership track. Although plans and policies are essential in creating a new framework – in other words, building new hardwiring to shift the culture of the institution – in reality, most of your career progression depends on the resources you can leverage. These resources are within your reach and range from relationships beyond your line manager to leaders with the ability to influence career decisions. Working hard and building luck is the balance between consistently demonstrating progress while ensuring you are in the line of vision when key decisions are being made around career opportunities. To get lucky in your career, there are some very specific areas to which you need to pay close attention:

- Visibility;
- Champions – relationships;
- Building self-efficacy – stretch opportunities;
- Shaping your leadership style.

Building visibility for your career is less about being in the right place at the right time and more about building a brand that is strong and reliable. Focusing on your leadership 'brand' may seem a bit cringeworthy and hyper-marketing for some of you, particularly if you strongly believe the quality of your work will speak for itself, but we feel it will give you a great template to build from. Think about shopping habits: how do you find out about new services or products? No matter how fantastic the offering is, often, without the targeted marketing through social media, endorsement or personal recommendations, you are unlikely to stumble across that special find. The marketplace is increasingly competitive and with high cross-global movement. In most countries and for many organizations, access to a wider global talent pool increases the ability to identify and draw the best resources, but it can also amplify the attitude of replacing talent easily rather than paying attention and investing in the current workforce.

Here's the paradox: the demand for more diverse candidates creates more opportunities for talented individuals to thrive in organizations, but at the same time the playing field has become more fragmented and far more competitive and requires different skills to progress. Raising your visibility is a multi-faceted approach and is based on certain requisites. Your work is consistently high quality, delivered on time and undeniably adds value to your team and wider organization. These conditions around delivery are non-negotiable and essential to ensure your promotion is earned, rather than being viewed as tokenistic or creating murmurings of promotion through entitlement. Meritocracy has to be the basis on which you develop and propel your career. This approach becomes your career DNA and the core of your strength. Your ability to acquire new skills and knowledge and agility to apply new thinking to different scenarios is key to your career development as we have consistently discussed throughout this book. In the same way, you need to think about yourself as software that needs updating to ensure the service offered is relevant and at the highest level.

The questions to ask yourself are: What is my unique service proposition (USP)?[69] What do I do that cannot be easily done by someone else? Your personal branding (USP) is more than your technical skills and experience, it is about your wisdom and knowledge made up of your wider experiences and perspectives combined with technical expertise. The more you expose yourself to building more lateral thinking, the more attractive you become for teams that aspire to have cognitive diversity at their core. How do you add value to improve the quality of thinking in the teams in which you work? Are you the person who challenges discussions through constructive dissent, to disrupt groupthink? In doing so, do you become the catalyst for the group to generate better-quality decisions and outcomes? People can get caught up in challenging, which can be seen as troublemaking, antagonistic or even aggressive, but when it occurs in a constructive and respectful manner, the outcomes are powerful.

In her seminal work on psychological safety, Professor Amy Edmondson of Harvard Business School showed that companies in which employees feel safe to speak out and voice concerns are actually the organizations that are more successful because they innovate better – so do feel

---

[69]You might be more familiar with 'unique selling point', but we prefer 'proposition' as this addresses a set of skills that combine to provide solutions.

positive about speaking out, but make sure you are doing so positively.[70] Or is your brand aligned with being the person who facilitates the team to get the task done, on time and under budget? Strong facilitation and project management skills are essential tools for career progression, but the risk for some (and often this applies to women) is that you become so entrenched as a team member, the risk of removing you for promotion is seen as too disruptive to the mechanics and that prevents it. The skill in building a personal brand demonstrates what you do well now but also the value of what you could do in the next role. This is more than dressing for the next role, it's about the value you bring to discussions, the insights you offer to leaders; it's also about how keen colleagues and leaders are to have you on their team. Being agile, co-operative and friendly might seem quite basic qualities but they are actually essential in how others view you.

Your external profile is equally important. As organizations become increasingly aware of their social media presence, the voices of individuals on social media are increasingly gaining attention. So what is your external presence? Above and beyond the cursory Google searches on you, what value does your social media profile add to your professional profile and how does it help to build your leadership image? Other questions to ask yourself: How often do you accept external speaking engagements? Do you use webinars or podcasts to raise your profile, build your network and create opportunities to share and shape your thinking? Returning

---

[70]https://hbr.org/podcast/2019/01/creating-psychological-safety-in-the-workplace

to Dame Inga Beale, she shares important tips for women building their leadership brand: 'I learned many years ago that there are many aspects to successfully navigating your career. A simple thing I did was to adopt the pie model – P.I.E. The "P" is for performance – you must perform well in your job. But also think about "I" the image – seek out feedback from others about how you are perceived and make sure that you come across in the way that you want to come across. "E" is for exposure – make sure you get involved in activities that go beyond your day job. Strategically work on your networks. Go out of your way to build new connections with people that you don't know and that you know could be influential in your career. But, above all, don't stay somewhere if the culture isn't right for you – it will inhibit your ability to flourish.'

Self-promotion on social media can sit uncomfortably for many of us, but if you have a strong sense of purpose, the attention becomes less about you as a personality and more about your messaging. We often hear talk of 'purpose' and we feel the critical piece underlying this is to have aims and motivation – it's the 'Results Focus' part of the dynamic careers model, but part of managing your career is knowing when to pivot, the 'resourceful mindedness' we discussed earlier (*see also* p. 155). This essentially boils down to the following: have ambition, drive and indeed, purpose and passion, but remember that needs to adapt to the environment. So, when you think about your goals in terms of achievements and what you want your career to look like in two, five or even 10 years, it's also important to consider the current turbulence and uncertainty impacting the world of work. This requires us to pivot by asking different questions: what is my purpose, what impact do I want to make in two/five or even 10 years and over the longer term, what is my legacy?

Focusing on your inner ambitions and drive allows you to step back from the day-to-day elements of what you are doing to create a more lateral approach to how you will get to your end goal. Furthermore, people are more willing to align themselves and invest in those who share a vision or sense of common purpose. Leadership for the sake of leadership is no longer attractive and will not build followers or individuals who are willing to invest in you and your dreams. Asking yourself what your purpose, drivers and ambitions are might be comfortable for some but deeply uncomfortable for many if it is the starting point. It's a good idea to consider why the discomfort or joy emerges as you ask the question. It's a question we often ask our MBA students, who have been working for 10–30 years and consistently their initial discomfort/interest comes from the recognition that they haven't considered this question since they were at school or university, making initial career decisions. It doesn't matter how long it's been since you've thought about this question, it matters that you spend some time thinking about it now. We're not advocating for you to make momentous, life-changing decisions, but in the face of tremendous change that requires reskilling or considering new career paths, isn't it better that you understand what drives you and how you can harness this for your career? More importantly, if you have a sense of the impact you want to make then you will find it easier to spot opportunities from the immense changes and transition into different paths more easily – this is how you get lucky.

It's all fine to talk about career progression but what happens when you are stuck, possibly with a line manager who is not as supportive about your aspirations? Breaking into new areas where there is great change can be difficult. Champions are powerful allies who can advocate for talent and give them a voice at the table. Stretch roles are equally important; a stretch role provides the opportunity for an individual to step out of their comfort zone and develop self-efficacy to propel their career further. In many cases for groups who are marginalized, champions provide access to these opportunities and talent guidance (Janjuha-Jivraj & Chisholm, 2015). The research showed that despite a clear leadership commitment to building a pipeline of female talent coupled with appropriate mechanisms such as training programmes and networks, the progression was slow and aspirations get stuck at a team level. Further investigation highlighted what is now commonly referred to as the sticky floor syndrome, where attitudes and behaviours of line managers subconsciously impeded progress for female team members[71]. The sticky floor is particularly challenging in career development. The attitudes that create barriers are due to subconscious biases and we've discussed the scale and impact of these biases on behaviour in Chapter 6 (*see also* pp. 117–138). With an even greater shift towards

---

[71]Baert, S., De Pauw, A.-S. & Deschacht, N. (2016). 'Do Employer Preferences Contribute to Sticky Floors?'. *ILR Review*. 69 (3): 714–736. doi:10.1177/0019793915625213.

distributed working patterns, the impact of line managers is seen as increasingly important and impactful on the outcomes of their teams. But, here's the tricky questions – what happens if you don't see eye to eye with your line manager and you're not convinced they will always act in your best interests?

In 2015, Shaheena led research on women leaders across 50 countries and found two common themes in the experiences of these extraordinary individuals: they had all been championed and had experienced stretch roles early on in new organizations.[72] This work was based on the Commonwealth countries, a remarkably diverse set of countries representing the polarized levels of economic, social and cultural differences. The women shared similar traits in behaviours – high achievement, endurance and stamina – but unfortunately, we know this is rarely enough to propel talented individuals into leadership roles. Challenging assumptions and biases can be difficult, if not impossible, if you don't have a group of individuals who are willing to challenge groupthink, being courageous to suggest alternative approaches and dispel long-held and often inaccurate assumptions. If you don't have a seat at the table, where is your voice? Who's going to advocate for you? Senior leaders with an explicit responsibility are essential to bring this perspective into decision making for new roles and opportunities. Championing enables this to happen and in the book, *Championing Women Leaders: Beyond*

---

[72]https://thecommonwealth.org/sites/default/files/inline/Women%20in%20
Leadership%20Discussion%20Paper.pdf

Sponsorship, Shaheena and Kitty explain the framework in which this support is important.[73] The CHAMP model addresses institutional barriers, along with personal barriers that prevent career progress:

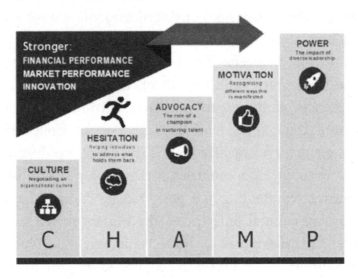

Source: Janjuha-Jivraj & Chisholm (2015)

While this framework was initially developed with a gender lens in 2015, more recently it has been applied in organizations that are committed to accelerating the advancement of individuals from minority ethnic backgrounds, along with women, into senior leadership.

Miranda Zhao, of Lloyds Banking Group identifies how championing is essential to build a strong pipeline of individuals who are under-represented: 'I think having a champion is a mental blanket. You know that your champion

---

[73]Janjuha-Jivraj, S. & Chisholm, K. *Championing Women Leaders.*

will give you the benefit of the doubt and see abilities that you may not have recognized in yourself. Once you feel that you have that trust with someone, who is higher up in the organization and that's willing to pull you up, then you're willing to take more risks, with yourself, your ideas and also take more risks and other people you want to pull up. So there's a bootstrapping effect. Then you also pay it forward; you do it to the next generation.'

Championing requires constant attention – it isn't a sheep dip and can't produce results immediately. Often, companies will state they have implemented sponsorship or championing programmes and despite starting with a great deal of enthusiasm, things wane and the programme stops. Championing needs a cohort of executive and senior leaders who are committed to investing in talent and proactively seeking opportunities for talented individuals (ones to watch); it also needs to be aligned to a wider and well-developed diversity and inclusion plan. In the championing framework, let's pay attention to the challenges around hesitancy – women in particular are often described as 'risk-averse'. The trait of risk-aversion is often used as a reason not to promote women into leadership or stretch roles. Risk aversion is often confused with ambiguity, with studies showing women are less willing to experience extended periods of ambiguity and will look to remove uncertainty.[74]

---

[74]Friedl, A., Ring, P. & Schmidt, U. (2017) 'Gender differences in ambiguity aversion under different outcome correlation structures.' *Theory & Decision*, 82; 211–219

Ambiguity around promotion and recruitment is often why women do not put themselves forward for stretch roles. However, this is often confused with women not being ambitious enough. The well-known study from Hewlett-Packard reminds us women will go for roles only when they feel they tick all the boxes in skills required, whereas their male counterparts will apply when they have just under half of the necessary skills.[75] A critique of the study by Tara Mohr identified the challenge among women applying for roles was not about confidence but about lack of clarity around the hiring process. The risk of failure was seen as wasted energy and time among women and reinforced the mistaken view that they are not hungry for stretch roles.

A further recruitment-based challenge that has impacted the progression of women is aligned to the attitudes towards recruitment decisions. A report written by Joanna Barsh for McKinsey's Centred Leadership research found that men are hired (or promoted) based on what they will do and in others, their potential, whereas women are promoted based on their track record and what they have already achieved.[76] If your organization doesn't have a clear championing initiative (this is not the same as a mentoring programme and should not be confused with mentoring), now is the time to start one. If you can't get a championing initiative set up, then create the next best

---

[75]https://hbr.org/2014/08/why-women-dont-apply-for-jobs-unless-theyre-100-qualified
[76]https://genius.com/Joanna-barsh-unlocking-the-full-potential-of-women-in-the-us-economy-annotated

thing: start building your network of leaders who are genuinely interested in promoting diverse talent.

Alongside championing, the other intervention essential to leadership progression is the opportunity for individuals to access stretch opportunities. Stretch roles provide an important opportunity for individuals to step out of their comfort zone and build confidence in areas that are new and challenging. They are essential for self-efficacy or confidence, described by psychologist Albert Bandura as 'an individual's belief in their ability to succeed in a particular task'[77]. Self-efficacy is intrinsic to individuals becoming successful leaders. Self-efficacy, or confidence, as it is commonly known, is one of the most enabling psychology models to have been adopted into positive psychology. It is the optimistic self-belief in our competence or chances of successfully accomplishing a task and producing a favourable outcome.

In the midst of even greater turbulence around careers, skills and leadership can be developed – possibly to a higher level. The pandemic, for example, gave leaders stretch opportunities – for even greater plasticity and adaptability to different contexts. This benefits every individual in a number of ways: first, they are far more comfortable working with colleagues from different divisions, disciplines and even sectors. In Chapter 6, we emphasized the importance of cognitive diversity – allowing yourself to be exposed to different opportunities, experiences and ideas that stretch your thinking. The benefits of working

---

[77]https://albertbandura.com/

in situations creating stretch, either in your experiences of delivery or building new ways of working with different individuals, provide the opportunity to create new neural connections. The confidence from achieving success in a role that is beyond your comfort level brings much more confidence and builds your appetite for even more stretch opportunities.

Being comfortable with uncertainty can provide you with more safety – paradoxical as it may seem. Humans find uncertainty uncomfortable but that uneasy feeling we often get when faced with potential change is from our evolutionary driver to make us seek certainty in new solutions. During uncertainty we become more critically observant and more vigilant of what is around us. This is a human trait to deal with danger. But by being observant of the people and climate around you, you can evaluate how taking a risk will impact. By being observant of what is within you, you can work out how to make the changes you need. By being mindful of your values, you can assess your ability and motivation to adapt. Marshall McLuhan (1911–80), the Canadian philosopher, in 1964 developed modern thinking on media theory (he was the person who coined the famous phrase 'the medium is the message'). McLuhan also discussed change and management of uncertainty and said: 'There is absolutely no inevitability as long as there is a willingness to contemplate what is happening.'

Playing it safe and keeping the status quo is comfortable but may not lead you to progress, but building new skills requires taking risks, which often feels very uncomfortable.

Becoming more comfortable with uncertainty is critical to leadership in the current age. As a leader, building your relationship with uncertainty can come from a systematic reconnection to your leadership purpose, understanding your values and regularly re-visualizing future plans.

CHAPTER ELEVEN

Summary: get bolder, braver

As we come to this final chapter of this book, we are pulling together the various elements to help you make sense of the key areas and where you need to pay attention to power up your leadership opportunities. There are some big messages but at the core of them is how you are able to develop yourself to adapt, flex and remain confident in your leadership. In the face of unprecedented change from emerging tech and wider societal shifts in the way we work, you as a person and your expectations of work and yourself will all continue to change as your life evolves and develops. One of our key messages is: keep ahead of the changes transforming organizations and functions. If not, then you could become a victim of change rather than navigating your leadership opportunities. By this point, you will have understood that the immense changes facing us provide significant opportunities and as we can see, the new frontiers of working also need different models of leadership. The question now is what will you do with the knowledge and perspectives we have shared with you?

In Chapter 1, we discussed the impact of wide-scale changes ahead of us due to new technology creating the fourth industrial revolution. At this stage it's not easy to fully understand the impact of these changes on our working lives, but we know from history that we navigate the seismic changes in economy and society by adapting and identifying emerging opportunities. In Chapter 2, we acknowledged the scale of uncertainty due to technology but also compounded by the impact of COVID-19. Becoming comfortable with uncertainty requires skill in continuous change and adaptability. Chapter 3 provided an overview of key trends in new frontiers of technology and how these innovations are likely to impact our world of work. Understanding the different categories of net technology can seem like a minefield, particularly if you are not a natural techie, however the quick guide in this chapter walked through the big trends. As you develop a better understanding of how the technology works and the principles underpinning development, it becomes far easier to relate to trends and opportunities that will impact your industry and even your function. As this chapter demonstrates, you don't need to understand how to write programs, but, like driving a car, while you don't need to know how internal combustion engines work, it's important to understand the principles to get the best out of technology. If, like us, you are inspired and excited by the impact of emerging AI on our world, then take this opportunity to dig deeper, find out who in your organization is championing AI and join in the conversations. As we've said over and over again, if you don't then the change will still plough on but you will be left wondering what in fact happened when everything around you has changed.

Chapter 4 – and the final element in the first section of our work together – mapped out why entrepreneurial leadership is the way for you to navigate your teams through the turbulence at work. New ways of working require new models of leadership; behaviours that encourage innovative thinking. The dominant leadership style from the Industrial Revolution stemmed from a highly autocratic and technocratic approach, which continued to dominate research for the next 80 years. The new paradigm of leadership builds on the value of collaboration and enabling teams to draw on diverse experiences and expertise to create new solutions. Leadership is now flexing to become more pluralistic to account for wider outcomes, including social and environmental impacts, as well as financial performance. While accountability still rests with the individual leader, their skill is more sophisticated in working with teams. Each person carries their own perspective on the changes ahead, but when these views are combined, the results are spectacular in providing even greater clarity around how to proceed.

In Chapter 5, we went into detail on resilience and used a research-based tool to enable us to manage our resilience better. We are still living with the impact of the global pandemic in both our personal and working lives and for many of us, the changes are still unfolding. It is likely the 2020s will be characterized as the decade of turbulence coupled with rapid adaptation. Building curiosity to welcome change means we need to get more comfortable with being 'stretchy'. As change accelerates, the idea of 'one job for life' will become outdated. We may not be used to this thinking as we have invested resources, time and energy in building a route for a successful career. These skills and training provide a strong foundation for us to continue learning and also the opportunity to pivot into completely new industries and roles, or make huge leaps in our existing areas to fall into synch with the impact of technology.

In the second part of the book, we focused specifically on you and your career, providing you with a leadership toolkit. Your career is important and building resilience (Chapter 5) is essential to handle the turbulence and growth you will need in order to flex. The key takeaway here is that nurturing and developing your leadership career is not a single one-off approach that only a rises when you are looking to make the next leap, instead it's a steeplechase and if you're not prepared for all the obstacles, you are more likely to fall at the first hurdle.

Chapter 6 on cognitive diversity explained why working within teams with different perspectives can be challenging if we use existing models of leadership and teamwork, but how through recognizing the limitations of social biases and nurturing a growth mindset, we are far more likely to embrace and celebrate different viewpoints and recognize the value they bring in creating innovative thinking.

Chapter 7 focused on a big area: learning to speak data as a business leader is critical and if you are a data geek, then it's equally important to get into the mindset of a business leader. The greatest risk for any organization is a lack of clear communication between business leaders and the data team and working on data in the absence of an ethical framework. The importance of creating narratives to connect wider stakeholders with important and new data-driven findings is more important than ever before for leaders.

Chapter 8 discussed the impact of career dynamism and deconstructing the core elements to help you maintain momentum. In particular, we focused on your drivers and the importance of dynamic capabilities in the workplace and how these apply to your career. We also focused on how activism is increasingly becoming an important element for your career progression.

In Chapter 9, we explained why learning and reskilling is your currency to stay relevant and able to renew yourself. Today, we have a wider choice of subjects and channels for learning than ever before, but with our crowded lives, it seems more difficult to commit the time to learning new skills. There is no getting away from it, we need to become very comfortable with ongoing or continuous learning as new skills are the currency to maintaining relevance in the next normal. We also highlighted the importance of meta-skilling.

Chapter 10, completing the second section of this book, focused specifically on skills you need to develop as leaders with regard to areas that have been recognized as essential resources to fast-track your career.

We have discussed at length that new technology will grow, but you as a leader need to focus even more on your ability to think critically about the adoption, so don't get into the hype and the tangles of various esoteric discussions, but focus on what you want to do/achieve. Ensure you start with the WHY before you go to the WHAT. For example, there is a greater pressure to develop AI that is 'explainable' (which means you can show-and-tell your algorithms, which may be harder than you'd like if you want to still innovate, but you'll need to balance innovation with safety) and you need to work out if this is critical, say to the building of your ethical AI strategy for your organization or sector.

A real and present danger is that the hype around new technology will mean that we move into technology and data-driven, not human-focused, leadership. The world of work is now people-driven, purpose-driven and mission-driven. Yes, of course businesses need to deliver financial and market success, but greater success is expected by ensuring that its impact on its people and the planet are also factored in. We also need to remember that business is a societal function – we are society and the *citizen worker* can change things. However, we do feel that there is a strong need for leaders to be not data-led but data-*informed* and so, it is important that we move to enable leaders to do well – by training and developing and building skills of empathy, along with analytical skills. Amateur managers are dangerous as overconfidence can mean decisions are not based on facts and data that go beyond a spreadsheet and machine learning. Developing the necessary capabilities to strengthen your entrepreneurial leadership is an iterative process throughout your career, where by you will not only gain experience but also wisdom in how you navigate yourself and your teams.

As we draw to a close with this book, we hope we have answered the questions you started with, but we are pretty certain you will have a new set of questions that need answering. If the closing questions are mostly about the 'whats' and 'hows', then we're on the right track. How many of these questions are churning in your mind: How do I find out about a new course I need to study? How do I find a champion? How do I broaden my network? How do I create stretch opportunities? We have provided you with information, encouraged you to question some of your assumptions and built in space for necessary self-reflection, equipping you with the ability to ask the important questions and determine the resources you need to keep moving. Remember, leadership is not a label, it's an activity, and you only hold the title when your behaviour and actions bring about change and mobilization of resources – it's a journey and it needs to be enjoyed.

Acknowledgements

Although this book has our names on the cover, there are so many people who have a hand in this project. This book first started as an idea in 2018 when we were part of the delivery team for an award-winning program for Women in Emerging Technology, between EY and Henley Business School. Claire Hewitt and Selma Turki, thank you for trusting us to shape the content which sparked this idea. The impact of the pandemic and first wave of lockdown created the perfect storm to decipher the implications of new technology on careers and ask critical questions about working in the new normal. We grabbed the opportunity to start working on the book. Writing a book is challenging, but we wrote while working from home, juggling the demands of home schooling, family needs, promotions, and an international relocation. Any one of these scenarios would have been challenging enough but combined we persevered with the support of family members, friends, and colleagues. So here's where we call out our heroes.

From Shaheena:

My gratitude starts with my husband, Zahir, my champion, for allowing me to nurture yet another spark. Education is given for a successful career, but the importance of a supportive partner can never be underestimated. He is a powerful role model to our boys, Iliyan, Kais and Zayn who provided humour and challenging conversations to keep this book alive. To the rest of my family, thank you for everything. Kitty Chisholm as always by my side, Stephane Dubois and

Karim Nanji for their immense support. Former colleagues from Henley Business School, the team on the Education Board and colleagues at HEC Paris, Qatar, particularly, Dean Pablo Martin de Holland for his patience as I moved into my new role while completing this book.

From Naeema:

There are four amazing people I want to acknowledge: my son Yusuf, as by some miracle he supported me in my dream of writing this book while achieving his own remarkable goals, and my nephews and niece Umar, Amaan and Zainab. They all inspire me because they not only inherited my intelligence, brilliant humour and modesty genes, they show me that while the world is changing fast, and the problems in it are challenging, their curiosity, courage and compassion shows our part in shaping a better world and excitement for the astonishing possibilities ahead. Massive thanks also to the wonderful people in Henley Business School who make me work harder and think better.

To all our contributors, who generously shared their insights on this area. You certainly challenged our thinking and your perspectives make the book so much richer and valuable to our readers.

To our students, we are so privileged to be part of your development and your growth as leaders in a constant source in inspiration. We hope you will recognize class discussions in the chapters.

Last but by no means least; to our amazing team at Bloomsbury: Matt James, Allie Collins, Amy Greaves; thank you for your patience, wisdom and humour.

Index

Note: page numbers in **bold** refer to diagrams, page numbers in *italics* refer to information contained in tables.